PHILADELPHIA
A Story Sequence in Verse

John Craig

Illustrations by Kevin Watts

Blue Logic Publications

BLUE LOGIC

2009

A Blue Logic Publication
P.O. Box 772
Oregon House, CA 95962
www.bluelogic.us

ISBN 978-0-578-04093-6

Printed in the United States of America

*This poem is dedicated to Victoria, my beloved wife,
who welcomed me to her city when I arrived.*

CONTENTS

AUTHOR'S NOTE

This poem is written in what I call, for lack of a better term, *catorzian meter*. Actually it's just a simple, fourteen syllable line. I find this meter has a wonderful flexibility and can serve lyric, narrative, dramatic and even epic aims. A catorzian line has the length to address serious thought and the suppleness with which one can hold conversation and engage in rhetorical play.

John Craig

Book One : *Daphne and the Dishes*

I.

"In the briefest or the most extended life, the moments
of lax inconsequence and nonevent outnumber far
the coiled-tight, compacted times from which we make our meaning.
And in a normal span, lived at an average distance
from history's attention, grand intensities comprise
a miniscule fraction, a waste of expectation's heat.
Our time is mostly trivial, measured in breaths and blinks.

II.

"To calculate how much of life is spent unremembered
is appalling, but here we are, between importances,
exhaling from the last stress, mounting to the next, waiting,
consolidating, glad to be of use to gravity.
Our last task done, our next not yet begun: the past recent,
the future near, where nothing yet moves by will, and time
escapes as unaccounted leakage of unnoticed air."

III.

Carroll paused, cleared his throat and adjusted his ample hips
in the parsimonious plastic chair. With true patience,
all around attended him to see if he had finished.
When he did not resume, Anamusa, her seat across
from his, smiled and spoke with frisky force. "What you say is true,
but Heaven does not leave us helpless, Carroll. Our bodies
sit marooned between events, but time is not our measure."

IV.

"So true," spoke Jules from Anamusa's left. "Time is not God.
It is the dimension of our words and thoughts, but not all—"
"The dimension of our rumps," Ruby blurted helplessly,
"in these inadequate chairs---oh, I interrupted you, Jules.
Please excuse me." She smiled straight across at him and lowered
her eyes in a brief intentional nod. Waiting to see
her eyes again, he smiled. "We do have time for each other."

V.

Jules continued, "Our bodies are in time; the truer part
need not be. All the bodily functions, from highest thoughts
to our lowest eliminations, from kind sympathies
to rude aggressions—all are movements circumscribed in time.
But to the soul they are but that—movements—as time itself
is movement, the traveling of mortal identities."
Ruby giggled at the irony of her discomfort.

VI.

"Yes, the effort to be out of time saves us," said Marco,
"when it works." He sat to Carroll's left, across from Mathilde,
his wife, who chimed, "It works when we work, Marco, does it not?"
"Precisely," Anamusa gleamed. "Efforts undertaken
seriously, and often enough initiated,
and held long enough cannot fail to take us out of time."
"If Heaven wills," politely interjected Jules with care.

VII.

"Behold the paradox we live," Carroll countered. "We aim
to spend as much time as we can out of time. Amusing."
"How else can we be comfortable in these carcasses?"
Ruby chortled as she crossed her legs. "Do you want to be
that tired, settling thing looking back from the bathroom mirror?"
All chuckled at her craggy comedy, each old enough
to have confirmed in the joints that life is transitory.

VIII.

"Friends, our lighthearted chatter on time is permissible
because the poignancy of what we know attends each breath
and thought, but our young auditor might be confused, troubled
at our frivolity. Let us speak as to include him."
Marco's admonishment brought a moment of still silence;
then all attention turned to me, and I felt in my cheeks
the flooding warmth of involuntary flush, and I coughed.

IX.

Anamusa gently said, "Please excuse us, William.
Our friendship is the fruit of an orchard tenderly groomed
for years, but we will gladly make space for a new planting."
A bright smile rose on Mathilde's often inscrutable face.
"What Ana says so well is true. Let us make room for him."
Marco was already fetching me a chair, which he placed
above the fixed and facing rows in which the others sat.

X.

I was suddenly in the middle of their charged array,
filtering every influence and feeling very young,
ill-fitted and exposed, though their heartfelt welcome calmed me.
I adjusted the chair to be aligned with the center,
almost between Marco and Mathilde, but leaving their view
of each other unblocked. I was the only one unpaired
but yet a true part of their ancient configuration.

XI.

And there we were, arranged in Heaven's order, delighted
in each other's company, awaiting flight home, while outside
the flaring lightening and exploding thunder threatened
all the sky. Hundreds milled about, sat, paced, chatted, read, dozed—
stranded in time—while we devised a story game to help
us hold the present and get something for ourselves, to help
us bring true worth to the airport in Philadelphia.

XII.

Though Carroll first proposed the game, he rightly credited
Chaucer, whose Canterbury pilgrims made their journey ripe
with every kind of story, each tale fitting the teller
in style and character. "Though not his numbers, his spirit
we have." Carroll claimed. "Each of us can surely tell a tale
or two before this noisy storm relents. We can enjoy
the narratives as well as what they show us of ourselves."

XIII.

"Are we really all storytellers?" wondered Jules, his face
betraying some unease. "The active ones speak easily,
as if walking or stirring soup, but I am slow to think
and talk, and when she utters words at all, Mathilde whispers
as softly as the hum of a moth's wings. Entertaining
such a group as we would challenge me, tax my present skill,
and send my tongue stumbling. Are we sure about this, Carroll?"

XIV.

"Beautifully said, Jules," Marco quipped, and the whole group flashed
a smile at Marco's gentle irony. "Like everything else,
it is an experiment. Let us see what we can do.
And more personally, from ten years of marriage to her,
I can promise you Mathilde can summon herself to say
whatever must be said." A stir of laughter shuffled through.
"Don't be over considerate, friends," Mathilde admonished.

XV.

"But I'm squeamish for a different reason." The blunt words
came from Ruby. "I know I have no story suitable
for this company. Before my call, I lived a rough life,
more a man's life, many years in uniform, brutal deeds,
raucous comradeship. My stories are the cactus apples
from this soil—some tragic, some raunchy, none dainty, none sweet.
My tales defy refinement and are better left untold."

XVI.

"Now this is an aesthetic problem," Carroll mused, stroking
his wispy beard. Where do things vulgar and violent fit,
if at all, in our game? The word 'obscene' derives from Greek
ob skena: acts too harsh for presentation on the stage
were done instead offstage and recounted by messenger.
But even there, with acts too bloody to be dramatized,
the tale of the act could be told. The words are not the deeds."

XVII.

"If Chaucer is our guide," Jules declared, "we need not tiptoe
past the vulgar." Anamusa joked with a foxy grin,
"Does this mean you're now a storyteller after all, Jules?"
"I still have reservations," Jules replied, "but our Chaucer
would dance past this problem with finesse. It's in the telling
whether a violent story is reverent or mean.
Even gross comedy can have a delicate stitching."

XVIII.

After a cordial silence, Anamusa cleared her throat
and spoke. "We have, remember friends, an aim to see ourselves.
When light is brought, the ugly crust of personality
disintegrates. It is embarrassing to watch oneself
reveling in violence, laughing loud at raunchy scenes,
but these parts of us must be seen. As we love each other,
we can profit from the meanest gift offered lovingly."

XIX.

"So it is true, we all agree," said Marco, looking round
at every set of eyes, searching kindly for objection.
"So be it," Jules consented. "If I stutter and stumble
over my words, I know you will forgive the clumsiness."
"And I will search my memory for something gossamer,"
said Ruby in accord, "though I'll be rummaging a room
of double steel-link and heavy canvas. I'll do my part."

XX.

"We do agree, " smiled Marco in delight. "Now, who begins?"
At that the unity began to strain, postures wilted,
and a chorus of light coughing and throaty rumbling rose
from the group. "If I'm to keep the promise I just made you,
I need a little time to think," said Ruby haltingly.
"Of course you do," chimed Jules, "as do I. Your idea, Carroll,
might best be served by your leadership. Would you like to start?"

XXI.

Said Carroll in sincerity, "I'll gladly be the first
to tell a tale, but can we not find a better reason,
a more intentional intelligence to our order?"
And Anamusa followed quickly on, "To trust the Gods
is good, but in this simple enterprise where our own lights
are sufficient, let us make an effort to establish
something exquisite. We have time for patience and beauty."

XXII.

Jules concurred, "Of course we do. My poor apprehensiveness
was speaking. Let us think to give our game a worthy form."
"I also spoke too soon, " admitted Marco. "Forgive me.
An indelicate rush of delight at this sweet prospect
swept me up. How easily forgotten is the conscious work
behind all good things. Let the next word said be wisdom's."
There followed a sure silence in the presence of themselves.

XXIII.

Some moments on, the next to speak was Carroll. "Does it not
matter less who will start than in what subsequent order
we proceed and what kinds of tales follow one another?"
"I beg your pardon," Ruby said and wide-eyed turned to Jules,
"what did he say?" Jules smiled and replied with seasoned calm.
"He said that anyone can begin, so long as what follows
is rightly ordered to law and, I presume, ascending."

XXIV.

"Ah", said Ruby, so unless I start, I follow Marco."
"Correct," Marco replied, "and I'd follow Anamusa,
as she follows Jules, who in turn awaits my dear Mathilde."
"And Carroll then is last?" burst Ruby in sincere surprise.
Jules reminded her, "Dear, we've yet to figure who will start."
Quietly Mathilde admonished them, "Forget not William."
"He can pick his spot, " concluded Carroll. "He blends in well."

XXV.

"But who will start?" piped Ruby with palpable persistence
but diminishing alarm. "I know I am not ready."
"The readiness is all," giggled Marco, reminding them.
Collecting himself, Carroll spoke with deliberate calm.
"When we rush, we disintegrate into mindless chatter.
Let us go about the careful business of our rules;
their structure will keep our bright game ascending, whoever starts."

XXVI.

At that moment on the tarmac just out of the window
facing Anamusa passed a luggage truck whose broadside
bore in wild graffiti, "*B-Luv rules!*" Anamusa read
and smiled and alerted the others who took the omen
quickly to heart. "The simplest rule is never to repeat.
Let each tale have its own theme, its own genre, polish, style,
its own illumination," asserted Anamusa.

XXVII.

"Yes, that's wise," said Marco, affirming Anamusa's plan.
"If each story is unique, competition can't intrude,
and our better goal remains before us." All but Ruby
seemed to share approving silence. "But what is that?" she asked,
and her boldness made me glad for I too had lost the thread.
"Why, to be out of time, my dear. Remember," Carroll urged,
"how this all began. Presence is the challenge of our game."

XXVIII.

"We'll tell our stories not first to entertain," chuckled Jules.
"Were that our real purpose, I would abdicate, protecting
 my slow and clumsy speaking skills from bare embarrassment.
"Yes," said Ruby, "thank you. I am reminded. But who starts?"
"If we could persevere with presence as you persevere
to know who starts, we would be flying now without the planes."
They all smiled at Carroll's jest as their minds returned to task.

XXIX.

"I think we all agree that repetition is a flaw,
and if we prize uniqueness, why not frame each tale?"
Each looked around the group for an understanding visage.
Said Carroll, "Please tell us what you mean by a frame, Marco."
"Is it like the ornamental boundary we construct
around a painting?" Anamusa asked. Mathilde was quick.
"A picture frame is so much more than ornament, my dear."

XXX.

"Indeed it is, " said Jules. A frame defines the space and keeps
the eyes from wandering. It calls one to right attention."
"Exactly!" Marco gleamed with animated smile. "It pulls
a clear image out of indistinction and presents it."
"If tales can also have a frame, " said Ruby, "tell me how."
"Do you mean a prologue and an epilogue?" asked Carroll.
"Yes, that," said Marco, "but with a specialized intention."

XXXI.

"And what's that intention? This simple game grows more complex
by the moment," Ruby lightly declared, not bewildered
but a little baffled. "What kind of framing would you have?"
"For instance," Marco said, "I'd like to hear how each teller
came by the tale he's telling. That's a story in itself."
Ruby brightened, "So you want a story round the story?"
"Thus the prologue," Carroll noted, "but how the epilogue?"

XXXII.

"Our minds have certainly grown active on this matter, friends.
The game has stirred us as a good game always stirs the mind.
Let us not forget it is a game, " said Anamusa.
"However we construct it, let us do so with the aim
of sustaining ourselves in the present." A pause ensued.
"The epilogue," said Marco with deliberate softness,
"should somehow bring the story here to Philadelphia."

XXXIII.

"So we carry it back to this group and deposit it
as the Phaiacians brought Odysseus home to Ithaca.
There will be," mused Carroll, "a delicate art to that work."
"So we have our form?" questioned Marco, his eyes surveying
all the faces of his fellows upturned in agreement.
"And now," Mathilde asserted, "we are a true colony
of our dear Teacher's art." "Yes," beamed Ruby, "but who will start?"

XXXIV.

As the growing crowd of waiting wayfarers milled about,
our gathering of kind friends continued the discussion.
Despite our tight array, we held discourse while indistinct
from the other men who, held by the magnetizing moon,
earth's grim gravity, nature's potent storm, their own bodies
and psychologies, believed themselves free-willed and unbound,
though currently unlucky, inconvenienced and stuck.

XXXV.

Hold this thought: the whole opera of human behavior
is done to enthrall; it is a grand, vacant deception,
a hologram. Those in it, who must believe, trust a cloud
of steam issuing into frigid air, disappearing
before it forms a meaning or an influence, its heat
gone, instantly dispersed, a comatose breath forgotten
and repeated till the thin film of life on earth is dry.

XXXVI.

And those separate in their knowledge, who do not believe
the human pageant, instructed men—we telling stories
in the airport—even we have scanty power to change
ends and outcomes. Our escape is of a different kind,
as each creates a soul, a self, a witness to this show,
a conscious being with whom the real Gods communicate,
and who receives from those kind Gods sustaining influence.

XXXVII.

By this distinction I remind you that what follows here
is not trivial. At times serious, at times comic,
now bright, now somber, I hope it is as edifying
and delightful as your wise heart can hold. But whatever
you think of the tales and their tellers, know that souls are growing
as the stories unfold, and attention well divided
between self and earthly fiction opens Heaven's own gate.

XXXVIII.

But who would start? That answer came in answer to a need.
As we'd agreed to frame each tale in yet another tale—
the story of the finding of the story being told—
we pondered what discovery would sound the brightest note,
thinking to begin with what attracted most our childlike
essences. With this aim came gentle pressure to decide
one's story, and the whole endeavor grew more definite.

XXXIX.

Of our seven, three thought to choose tales from real childhood.
Ruby, still believing her adulthood furnished nothing
properly refined, searched her mind for girlhood's wonderments—
but alas, the lock on memory's treasury refused
to yield, and she was left in longing for something waiting
there—she was so sure—but inaccessible to her. So clear
the failure of her search, so firm, that she came quickly home.

XL.

And Jules as well searched his childhood—the nightly narratives
his parents, one or the other, offered at his bedside,
and those of his own first readings, when reading was itself
a mystery, where each new clue surprised a dewy mind.
And what he found was all Andersen, the master, whose tales
this company would all know well already, but he thought
to contrive a tribute tale, following the master's lead.

XLI.

But as he wondered which familiar plot could best extend
to sequel, dear Mathilde dissolved the cloud of pondering
with words both mild and absolutely sure. "I will begin."
Our company quickened to attend her, relieved, feeling
in her declaration's clear command an interval bridged
and closed. "Is your story from your childhood?" Carroll queried.
Mathilde smiled, "From my childhood, yes, but strangely not of it."

XLII.

"Ah, this is good," Jules opined, "for I think I'll be ready
to follow Mathilde with a tale sibling to one we know."
"Sibling meaning 'in the manner of'?" Anamusa asked.
"A sequel to a fine one by the master," Jules replied.
"Chaucer, Cervantes, Shakespeare, Andersen, Lewis Carroll--
we all know stories from all of them. Whom do you mean, Jules?"
"Each childhood its magician, Marco. Mine, Andersen."

XLIII.

"And I'll follow Jules with a mythic tale in the Greek style,"
Anamusa claimed. "Mythic tale?" Ruby wondered aloud.
"Perhaps as told by Ovid," suggested Carroll smartly.
"We're getting ahead of ourselves, darlings," Ruby advised,
"but it sounds like we're in for a bit of a sit. I'll be back."
"Let's adjourn to the present," smiled Mathilde, "reassembling
here after looking briefly to our comfort." All agreed.

XLIV.

In Philadelphia, nothing is so common as the face
of Benjamin Franklin, and as we friends moved down the hall
to restrooms and the coffee bar, Franklin's wise countenance
on a mortgage company's billboard provided us all
a blessing: with his face the words, "Well begun is half done."
Soon refreshed, renewed in our configuration, we sat
aware of our attention to Mathilde who thus began.

XLV.

"Everything I now am begins with my grandmere, Mami,
my mother's mother, whom I trusted like a deity
to tell me the plain truth and explain the world's mystery.
She lived with us through all my childhood, and her influence
guided the growth of my young mind and heart. My allegiance
to her was unbreakable, and in return she gave me
the form of wisdom. How do girls grow up without grandmeres?

XLVI.

"A daughter is her mother's for three years, wherein the babe
absorbs the arduous love and pertinent hardiness
life on earth requires from mother. She learns instinctively--
though not without delight—the web and weight of living.
But this custodial time dissolves, as the budding mind
of childhood then thirsts to learn the language and attention
which is humankind's alone. Here the patient grandmother.

XLVII.

"A thousand questions: What is this? Who is that? Why can't I?
To know me now, you might not think that I was full of words,
an endless flow that only a grandmere could tolerate.
Not knowledge, but a certain kind of sharing was the aim,
though I was blank about it then. The words were functional,
to decorate time, but nurturing camaraderie fed
Mami's delight in me and my delight in novelty.

XLVIII.

"The mornings, when our minds were freshest, we would spend in games
of learning. Whatever were my questions, she'd transform them
to adventures, and off we'd go to Papa's library
to search, but also the church and the shops in town.
By four I knew my alphabet and could spell many words,
but my letters, as if tumbling from a box, were clumsy
and all over themselves. The fat crayons smudged my fingers.

XLVIX.

"And afternoons were for the fingers. I mean we made things.
She would knit or sew—always something in the works for me
or Mama—and I would string beads for a necklace or cut
snowflakes or fingerpaint the dark forest and the strange light
beyond it coming through, myself in the foreground peering
in and wondering. Mami played piano and taught me
sweet songs, but all I wanted of music was to listen.

L.

"At three we took a nap, though I admit that many times
I did not sleep but rode the waves of Mami's long breathings
to imaginary destinations where I waited,
thought and made up conversations—another kind of sleep.
At four we did our stretches—long slow poses so easy
for young bodies I hardly thought them exercise at all.
'The habit of suppleness,' Mami'd say, 'defeats habit.'

LI.

"From then till dinner, we'd sit by Mama's flower garden—
or indoors by the fire in cool months—chattering like birds.
Mami was deeply Christian, and she hoped that I would be.
If no child's topic claimed the hour before Papa returned,
Mami would proffer questions about Jesus, not to teach
overtly but to pique my curiosity and turn
toward Heaven my baby mind which hardly knew up from down.

LII.

"'Why does Jesus love you?' she would ask most often, and I
would give one silly answer or another, as I knew
so well the phrase she sought. 'Because he's nice and good to all,'
I'd say most any day, but on an impish day I'd say,
'Because I'm pretty.' And then with a smile only Mami had,
a smile gentle as clear water in a slow running stream,
she'd say, 'Because he's love.' I did not understand for years.

LIII.

"Papa arrived a little after six and soon we'd dine.
I listened to their old talk, pretending to understand,
ignoring all the words I didn't know or making up
a meaning, wanting to be part and growing quickly tired
in that heavy work. Long before Papa had spent his day's
full gravity of words, I could not lift my fork. My lips
were freighted with sleepy profundity. Time slowed and drooped.

LIV.

"The bedroom soon was there, and I, revived some, would prepare
for the day's last delight. I don't mean prayers, for by then thoughts
were heavy clothes, and thinking what to pray was like ballet
in an overcoat. I mean the story Mami'd daily
conjure from the ethereal library in her brain.
I'd settle into bed in sweet expectation, certain
of news from a fairy kingdom or a new friend to meet.

LV.

"We had a little ritual. 'Good evening, miss,' she'd say,
and I'd reply, 'Good evening, Mami.' Then she solemnly
would ask, 'Are we ready now to close this (whatever) day
of (whatever) month?' and I'd answer, 'Let us close it well.'
'And how do we do that, Mathilde? How is the day well closed?'
'I know!' I'd say, almost before her question left her lips.
'I pledge to truly listen to the tale you choose to tell.'

LVI.

"And then she would begin, 'Once in the peppery kingdom,'
or 'Once on a ship in the sea of resentment,' and then
she'd stop and look down at me, her eyes intently on mine.
'Are we keeping our pledge, Miss Mathilde? To listen truly
means much more than with the ears, but with the whole heart and mind.'
'I am listening, Mami. I know that I am,' I'd say.
Then would unfold half an hour of Heaven's best magic.

LVII.

"There followed instant travel unimpinged by time or space.
Back to sandy pyramids we'd go where lion men sat
in perfect passive comprehension, or to the temples,
groves and theatres of Greece, or to ever-marching Rome's
most horrible displays. Crusaders and conquistadors
drove their armored horses by in urgent headlong charges,
and ladies of all eras watched helpless at high windows.

LVIII.

"But I exaggerate. Mami's fanciful histories
were like the plots of operas. Riding on the drama
and the ritual of telling, I would clutch the bedsheets
till my exhausted grip gave way and I fell into sleep.
I rarely lasted through a whole heroic narrative,
but my dreams those nights were noisy, and later when I went
to school, I marveled how inaudible was history.

LIX.

"But Mami sometimes told a more delightful kind of tale
with a sweeter destination—the forest magical,
or so I called it: to her it was an enchanted place
of all possibility which I chose as a forest.
Let me explain. In this kind of tale, the teller conspires
with the listeners. The teller spins the yarn out but stops
at crucial intervals for listeners to intervene.

LX.

"So Mami would begin, 'This story has its setting in—'
then she'd stop and look at me in silent expectation.
'The forest magical!' I'd always beamingly exclaim.
She'd continue, 'And into that enchanted place where all
the laws of freighted flesh collapse in present wonder walked--'
Now Daphne was my made-up name, so 'Daphne!' I would squeal.
Now while we wait, I'll tell you all my favorite forest tale.

LXI.

"Mami adjusted herself in her chair and settled in
for her telling while I readied my happy attention.
'Daphne did not deliberate at all but marched right in,
trusting the protection of an invisible spirit
she'd always assumed watched over her. For many meters
the forest was not deep or dense, and though each tree was grand,
the whole was as sparse as the hair on a grandfather's head.

LXII.

"'Unbroken streams of light flowed in; the puny shadows hid
themselves and trembled. The fat birds in their indolence said
little, and nothing musical. The leafy ground was firm.
Short of a hundred steps, Daphne paused to wonder aloud,
'Why would my mother, who is not a silly woman, warn
me not to enter here? It is not dark. It is not far.
Turning around, I can still see smoke from our chimney.'

LXIII.

"'She turned and searched the sky. 'Well, perhaps they've finished cooking.
At any rate, I'm going on. I yet will hear the bell
my mother rings to call me back.' So on she pranced and skipped,
fell lightly once or twice—no blood or bruises—noting not
the deepening shade. What stopped her was a long throaty yawn—
or was it a roar? —ahead in misty distance darkened
by thickening foliage. Was it the sound of sleep or pain?

LXIV.

"'How had she missed those shrieking jays, and what was brushing now
against her leg with every step? How soft the rustling ground!
It must be noon, but where's the sun? The trees had closed their ranks,
joined arms, and huddled over her in observation rapt.
The mist became an all-enveloping fog, yet tender
stayed her heart, not panicked but accepting, and within her
no thought of retreat or return. Reduced to fact, she stopped.

LXV.

"'Determined to determine where she was, she listened and looked
with quickened eyes and ears. She could see nothing but vapor.
When she extended her arm, her hand vanished in the fog.
Yet the low roaring noise was now distinct: neither human
nor animal, but a mighty flush of rushing water.
As clarity appears like bravery but is finer,
she started toward the roar with steps directed by her ears.

LXVI.

"'As her strides grew more resolute and rhythmical, the fog
thinned and stole away, and in a space not measured by time
but by advancing certainty, she arrived at the bank
of the deepest, fastest frothing rapids she could take in
with her senses. An impression unimaginable!
It was a marvelous boundary, but she marveled more
that she had no fear in her heart. Now, how to get across?

LXVII.

"'As she moved down from the rocky bank to the water's edge,
she realized the channel was not full but could yet hold
three meters more of flooding torrent. 'Whatever you are,
thank you,' she thought, 'for making this crossing more possible.'
Something in her understood that gratitude was helpful
as it made her feel guided, invited to this threshold
and beyond. 'Now,' she asked with earnest gaze, 'where are the rocks?'

LXVIII.

"Here I had to interrupt. 'Mami, how could Daphne know
that there were rocks?' She answered sans a pause and then resumed,
'Because she could not walk on water yet, of course. Attend.
She counted one…two…three…four…five…How many all in all?'
"Six," I blurted. 'And why six?' she asked, her brows firmly arched.
'Only six rocks for such a wide channel? Can you be sure?'
"She'll just have to be a bold girl and make some leaps," I said.

LXIX.

"'So she will. And so she did until she found herself held
fast on the sixth rock with four frothing meters left to leap.
'What now?' 'A fish?' I asked. 'No, when the waters are churning,
the fish are rarely friendly.' I brightened. 'Perhaps a branch?'
'From an overhanging tree, you mean?' 'Yes, I think I do.'
'Resourceful Daphne then received the soft, extended arm
of a shorewatch willow which swung her lightly to the bank.

LXX.

"'The touching of her feet to earth elicited a sense
of brave accomplishment which she knew she must not savor.
'How strange,' she thought, 'as I did nothing but to grasp the branch
extended to me. Yes, I saw it, but my eyes were not
looking for it…. I must wonder about this later on.'
An urgency that thought could not resist drove her feet up
the bank where the forest resumed, still dense but fogless now.

LXXI.

"'She moved at less than a run but more than a skip, darting
around thick trunks and ducking low hanging foliage dappled
by the welcome light. Her unpiloted repeating bounds
transformed to joyous choreography to which each apt
and eager muscle lent its thrusts and turns. Onward, onward
till all in her was spent and a heated harness tightened
round her chest and halted her, panting, just beyond delight.

LXXII.

"'With slow, deliberate footfalls and telescoping gaze
measuring the space around, Daphne let her lungs freely
gulp the air as she took her bearings, though having no clue
what her bearings determined. Ahead a hundred meters
was a pool of light, a clearing, and four wispy columns
of white smoke, evenly spaced across her field of vision.
She did not hesitate but knew her full foot with each step.

LXXIII.

"'Into the clearing she walked as into the market place
of her town. There before her, evenly spaced left to right,
were four tents, each with a little fire in front, attended
by a human figure. As she approached, in unison
they motioned to a flat and polished stone before them,
centered and elevated one full step above the ground.
'Stand there,' they said as one. 'Step up, and from there see and hear.'

LXXIV.

"'Gingerly but without fear, dear Daphne mounted the stone.
At once the figure far left began to speak, standing up,
unwinding from what had been a cramped, cross-legged posture.
'My tent is poor, often collapses in the wind; my clothing
poorer still, for as you see I naked am. I know not
what nourishment will drop into my bowl each day, and yet
I am content. I offer you a life absolved from fear.'

LXXV.

"'Unwisely fearless are the innocent, so says Mama,'
Daphne nodded. Without complaint, the figure refolded
and resumed his meditation of the fire before him.
As if she knew the ritual, Daphne moved her focus
right to the next fire. A smallish woman draped head to foot
in folds of fabric white and black began a rhythmic chant
and swung a censer back and forth that gave off sweetened smoke.

LXXVI.

"'On finishing her stark enchanting syllables, she spoke.
'Though I own nothing, my rare raiment and my domicile
are glorious in dignity, my life a constant prayer
of love's obedience. My thoughts are mastered, some say starved,
but I am free of a troubled mind, and my heart expands
to find everywhere the brim of God's infinite chalice.
I offer you the chaste submission to God's perfect love.'

LXXVII.

"'From within her tent, which now appeared as the humble front
of a splendid pavilion, the inspired polyphonies
of a selfless choir wafted out to Daphne and kissed her
breathless with seductive promise. She had no argument,
no words, but knew she could not rest there in the woman's gaze.
With stronger force of will than yet had been required of her,
Daphne turned away and directed her attention right.

LXXVIII.

"'The third fire smoldered unattended before a drab tent,
patched and shiny-worn in spots but not unclean nor seedy.
Beside the tent stood a sturdy desk piled high with parchments,
maps and charts and stacks of books that barely left the thin man
visible there, stooped over, nose to text, his scalp skin shining
through his thinning hair. Distractedly he rose, stared her way,
eyes hugely magnified by heavy spectacles, and spoke.

LXXIX.

"'Are you here for knowledge?' Daphne simply looked, carefully,
at the whole strange picture, moving her eyes over the scene.
'Perhaps I am,' she replied at last with sincerity,
'but are you not concerned your fire will die? It barely smokes.'
'It takes some work,' admitted the frail fellow, 'but each night
I get it strong enough to read by.' 'And what do you read?
Those charts and parchments on your desk, I'd guess.' Daphne pointed.

LXXX.

"'Pointing leaves you unprepared, my dear, and guessing is worse.
These things on my desk are but this moment's calculations.
Here's the real point.' He moved to his tent, clasped the entrance flap
and with an awkward flourish held it open wide for her.
There stretching back as far as she could see, meters or miles,
were books, stacks upon stacks, a dense faint-lit forest of books.
Daphne stood amazed. 'What does one do with all that knowledge?'

LXXXI.

"'The question had jumped from her like a fish breaking a pool's
smooth surface to its own surprise. 'What do I do with it?'
His eyes, showing red at the rims, bulged behind the lenses.
'Why, my dear,' he continued, 'can you not see? I stack it.
It's all precisely organized by a great plan devised
over decades: the master taxonomy of knowledge
taxonomies—the key to it all. And you can learn it.'

LXXXII.

"'Daphne's heart sank and she slumped back off the stone, bewildered.
She gave one last plaintive look to the thin man of knowledge
closing his tent. With a nod he directed her eyes right.
'Try him,' he said. At this point I could not help breaking in.
'Mami, I am lost in this mystery. Is there something
Daphne must recognize? Does she know what she's meant to find?'
Scanning her thoughts with great care, she plucked an answer for me.

LXXXIII.

"'The man in the farthest tent awaits us. Now what is he?'
'He's an unknown magician,' I said, the words having life
all their own, for no thought in my head had ushered them forth.
'And what are his features?' she asked, bending close to my eyes
with a gaze open as the universe and welcoming.
Again the words issued from me, 'He's bald and frightening
and gruff, but his eyes say, 'Fear me, Daphne, and you lose all.''

LXXXIV.

"Mami sat silent a moment. 'Mathilde, my dear darling,
the rest of the story is yours to tell me, though the words
will come from my lips. 'But Mami, I don't understand you.
Am I sleeping now and dreaming?' The story went right on.
'You're the unknown magician,' said Daphne in bold approach.
'I can't be unknown if you know me.' His gravel-throated
gruff reply scratched the air as he warmed his water for tea.

LXXXV.

"'Ah, tea,' said Daphne delighted. 'Is there enough for me?'
'Tea, yes, but time, no.' he said in a growl. 'You must get on.'
'And where am I going?' Daphne indignantly queried.
'Not where,' he barked, but who. Who?' He held her eyes in his own.
'Who am I going?' asked Daphne in naïve confusion.
'To be,' came his gusty whisper. She fought to hold her mind.
'Who am I going to be?' 'Go see,' said the magician.

LXXXVI.

"He reached his left arm behind him and pointed through the trees
to a distant hill. 'Over that,' was all he said, and raised
his finger toward the sky. Her gaze ascended to the clouds
above the hill, to one which swirled up from its billowed base
as a sheer spiral staircase climbs a castle watchtower.
'Farewell,' his raspy whisper said. 'And what of you?' she asked.
'Excellent tea is enough for me now. Go find your way.'

LXXXVII.

"'But alone?' said Daphne mournfully. 'Must I go alone?'
'You're the only one who thinks so. What help you need will come.'
'I don't understand,' she pouted. 'Then that's the help you'll get,'
he said with uncompromise, 'just as I need your help now.'
The steaming water went into the waiting glass, making
a fine aroma. 'But how can I possibly help you?'
'I drink my tea attending silence.' Daphne understood.

LXXXVIII.

"'Then I'll go and not be afraid,' she said turning, but then—
'I've one last question. Are you really a magician, sir?'
'What is your attention doing now?' he huskily asked.
A presence grew from behind her eyes, animating her
and showing forth. 'This is one strange business you're in,' she gleamed.
'But a very profitable one,' whispered he, sipping
artfully from his glass. 'To your silence,' she said, turning.

LXXXIX.

"Having a destination but no particular route,
Daphne proceeded on the assumption she would get there.
Though there was much more forest between her and it, the hill
rose clear above, rocky and bald of all vegetation.
She began a straight path with a high heart, but quickly found
the forest to be more than trees, but a tangle of vines,
outcroppings, creeks and moraines that allowed no straight pathway.

XC.

"She had zigged and zagged for half an hour when she realized
the top of the hill could no longer be seen. Where was it,
and where was she on this trip to finding out who she is?
Being lost was everywhere, and she almost believed it.
'There's a hill up there somewhere,' she reasoned, 'could I but see
over these rocks and trees.' 'You could climb,' said a kindly voice
which she assumed had come up from her own inner chatter.

XCI.

"'I could,' said Daphne, deep in thought, 'but in this dress the bark
would slice my legs to coleslaw.' ' Then how 'bout a rocky mound?
Not as tall, but some elevation is better than none.'
'This is true,' Daphne thought, or said—she wasn't sure. 'I'll find one.'
'There to your left just past that small grove,' the kindly voice said.
'Why, thank you,' said she, turning her head in that direction.
She took a step and stopped. 'But whom have I been speaking to?'

XCII.

"'Are you asking who I am?' asked the voice. 'Shall I tell you?'
'What I really mean, I think, is that I'd like to see you.
A voice one cannot see is an eerie thing,' said Daphne.
'Ah, but even if I stand before you hiding nothing,
you will not see my voice,' the kindly voice reminded her.
'You know what I mean,' she firmly said, planting her small feet.
'People often tell me that. I wish I could be so sure.'

XCIII.

"'Sure of what?' said Daphne, growing indignant. 'That I do
in fact know what they mean. It seems to me quite uncertain.'
The voice spoke in calm resignation. Some branches rustled.
'That must be you,' she said to the staunch figure exiting
the foliage. 'Must it be?' he said, coming into the light.
Daphne'd had enough. 'Are you being profound or stupid,
or perhaps both, you not-bad-looking middle aged man, you?'

XCIV.

"She spoke the final 'you' as emphatic accusation.
He approached with a drastic limp that Daphne pained to see,
but the brave smile never left his face. 'Permit me,' he said,
'I am The Crippled Knight of Clear Thinking.' He bowed with care.
'Thank you, finally,' said she. 'I'm Daphne, with no title.
I've lost the hill I'm looking to get over in order
to find the place I'm supposed to be.' He replied, 'I know.'

XCV.

"'How do you know/' she asked, chafing a bit, then thought better.
'Never mind,' she said. 'If I ask you, you'll just say something
even more annoying, won't you?' 'With you as you are now,'
he said brightly, 'I'd have no choice. Annoyance feeds itself.'
Daphne stopped talking and felt the uncomfortable heat
in her face. She stood there quite fixed and breathed deeply, letting
the hot blood retreat. 'Sorry,' she said. 'Well done,' he replied.

XCVI.

"'Now,' she said, 'back to the elevation, your rocky mound.'
'I assure you, it isn't mine. I own almost nothing.'
'Here we go again,' she warned. 'You're right,' he said. 'I must learn
to pay much less attention to what is actually said.'
'Or more to what is actually meant,' suggested Daphne.
'That would require years of development.' 'So long?' she mused,
striking off for the mound and bounding bravely to the top.

XCVII.

"'I'm afraid so,' he confessed. 'Don't be afraid,' she giggled,
pointing with her full arm. 'Our hill! I see its balding top!
'Line it up with something higher,' he instructed wisely.
'Like the sun?' she inquired. 'No, dear, the sun moves. Something fixed.'
'But there's nothing fixed and higher I can see,' she explained.
'A delicious irony,' he almost sang. 'No fixed stars
in the daytime, and at night one can't see one's next footfall.'

XCVIII.

"'So what now?' she asked. 'Something beyond irony, at least.
Of that I'm almost sure,' he affirmed. 'Clear thinking?' she asked,
smiling down on him with innocent delight and warm heart.
He smiled back with equal gladness, asking 'What do you see
between here and the hill?' 'Nothing but treetops,' she answered.
'Are all the trees the same?' 'They look like a carpet from here.'
'What do you see behind you?' he asked, patience presiding.

XCIX.

"'I could say I can't see behind me,' she laughed, 'but I know
what you mean.' She turned round and scanned the distance dutifully.
'The same,' she called, turning back to fix her gaze on the hill.
'But you know,' she said in slow discovery, 'there's an edge
far out to the right. A border, I mean, where the trees end.
It looks as if we can reach the hill by a long way round.'
She traced the air. 'First back right, then a long trek round, then left.'

C.

"'How often we humans come to ourselves before a choice,'
said The Crippled Knight with a knowing look at Daphne.
'What choice, sir?' she asked. 'Why plunging blindly through with high
hopes to find our summit, or marching the many extra miles
more certainty requires.' 'Well, sir, I am young. I have time
to take the surer way, but you are troubled in the leg
and may prefer a headlong risk to an enduring labor.'

CI.

"'Are you saying you'd dismiss your better inclination
just to go with me?' Daphne firmed. 'No, that's not what I mean.
I beg your pardon, sir. I was trying to determine
too delicately if we are to go on together
or wave to separate plans. The path of perseverance
is the wiser choice for me.' 'You are right, my dear,' he said,
smiling within, 'though not so young as you think. Let us go.'

CII.

"So they set off, back through the trees to the forest's border,
a brief passage but quite perilous for the limping knight
who stumbled and slipped but bore the tree-crowded, rocky slopes
with no betrayal of ill humor. Daphne, for her part,
slowed her pace, resisted the urge to bound o'er the terrain,
and watched to see the good hero didn't take a tumble.
When the trees were behind them, they were bonded in their task.

CIII.

"They walked more easily now, a gently ascending way,
almost a road compared to where they'd been, the hill ahead
more distant but in clear sight. As they went, she questioned him.
'So what lies o'er the hill, old knight? You've been there, I suppose.'
'Oh, yes. It's a wonderful place for work and for striving.
So beautiful. I can't think of a better place for you.'
'Now wait,' she upstarted. How can you know what's good for me?'

CIV.

"'That's not difficult, my dear. Now tell me, what do you want?'
Daphne wriggled her nose. 'What do you mean, what do I want?'
'I mean, what's the most important thing?' he asked, looking her
straight in the eye. 'The thing on which all else in life depends.'
'Truth!' she exclaimed, feeling the word enter her mouth and hearing
it fly out without ever having been a clear thought.
Daphne covered her mouth in amazement. 'Did I say that?'

CV.

"'In a way. It was, after all, your mouth that issued it.'
'Am I right?' she asked sincerely. 'One kind of right,' he gleamed.
'You might have answered love or beauty or understanding,
but in the end, they are all one. With truth, you'll get them all.'
'How wonderful!' she gushed. 'And freedom. Do I get that too?
It means a lot to me now that I can do what I want.'
'Ah,' he laughed, 'there's your youth at last. I wondered where it was.'

CVI.

"'Is there anything wrong with wanting to be free?' Daphne asked,
a bit piqued. 'Not wrong, but adolescent,' chortled the knight.
Without meaning to, Daphne accelerated her pace
and strode ahead, but he maintained his even-labored limp.
After a few tense seconds, she turned and confronted him.
'I want to be free,' she asserted. 'You are free,' he smiled,
'but freedom serves only those who want the good. Is that you?'

CVII.

"She waited and pondered as he hobbled up beside her.
Catching her eye, he said, 'Now you're stopped in thought, but with work
we'll have you in stopped thought.' Her face contorted in puzzlement;
serene love attended his eyes and softened his voice.
'Do you want the good?' he asked. 'My heart says yes,' she trembled,
but first I must know the good.' The pools of her eyes were still.
Once more he smiled within and touched her head saying, 'Onward.'

CVIII.

"They moved on deliberately, their talk alternating
with moderate passages of delectable silence.
The questions rose in her like divers seeking the surface,
but she resisted venting every thought, kept some control.
Only those matters that pressed repeatedly found their way out,
and he would patiently direct her questions, not always
answering them but showing how they were best thought about.

CIX.

"After two hours at their steady pace, the bald hill had grown
prominent in sight, and in cheerful fatigue, Daphne's thoughts
settled to queries more personal to her companion.
'Are you really a knight?' she asked, at last surrendering
to curiosity. 'I mean, you're nicely dressed and groomed,
but you're unarmed, and why would a knight be walking alone
in the woods? One would think you'd have something better to do.'

CX.

"'But are you not a damsel in distress?' he asked calmly.
'Am I old enough to be a damsel?' she asked, surprised
and a bit proud, but just as quickly turning indignant.
'But I was not distressed. When we came upon each other,
I was somewhat confused, but I knew where I was going.'
'Forgive me,' he said softly. 'Far be it from me to think
that I could rescue you. I'm just glad for the company.'

CXI.

"'But are you a true knight?' she asked again. 'For if you are,
show me your sword, your lance, your horse, your bold insignia.
Whom do you represent? Who made you a knight? What kingdom
do you serve?' she persisted. 'What kind of quest are you on?'
He smiled as his mind transformed the questions into a way
of instruction, and his legs and back enjoyed the brief pause.
'For a knight of my order, the quest is always the same.'

CXII.

"'And what is it?' she pressed him in misconceived advantage.
'The quest of the moment,' he answered. 'Is that like the soup
of the day?' she said archly. 'What's the quest of the moment?'
'The moment,' he replied. 'Yes, but what is it now?' she cried.
'Precisely now,' he reassured. 'Find your feet as you talk.'
She was flustered and again indignant. 'Here are my feet,'
she bristled, 'and you are the unkind knight of confusion.'

CXIII.

"'Oh, my,' he sighed. 'I'm just going to quit talking,' she said.
They walked on in silence, the sun now high and hot, the way
a narrow, rocky, welcome edge coiled around the forest.
'I'm glad for this path,' he said at last. She did not reply.
No more in steady ascent, the rugged way turned sharply
in steep decline, more difficult for the crippled hero,
toward the bald hill's massive base. 'Summon yourself now,' he warned.

CXIV.

"She broke her silence. 'It's all downhill from here. The work's done.'
'Not exactly,' he admonished as his footing struggled.
Unwillingly accelerating, the knight stayed upright
only with the greatest toil, and soon he was advancing
in headlong rush toward the rock at the path's brute end.
With five meters to go, his stretched his bad leg out and whirled
his bold momentum in a perfect pirouette and stopped.

CXV.

"He faced her now, and with the slightest bowing of his head
and a sincere smile said, ' Here we are.' She looked down at him.
'Fine time to be dancing,' she said, as she effortlessly
shuffled up beside him. 'What now?' 'Precisely,' he replied.
'But where do we go from here?' 'Nowhere,' he said, his visage
turning serious. 'That is, *we* aren't going anywhere.
Here we split—you to go over the hill and I to home.'

CXVI.

"She felt a sudden chill. 'But how am I to overcome
this massive rock? It's almost straight up.' An urge to whimper
rose in her, a temptation to enact the helpless child.
'There is a way,' he said calmly. 'Fifty meters back up,
you'll find an ancient cut going all the way to the top.
It was formed by the patient action of a rivulet
over centuries, just for you, Daphne, to climb today.'

CXVII.

"Her sudden trepidation turned with equal suddenness
to red-faced irritation. 'How can you know that?' she fumed.
'Come to think of it, how did you know my destination?
Did I tell you? Didn't I? What is happening to me?'
She felt her anger melt into the prompting of a sob.
He did not speak but gave out a high melodic whistle
and soon was heard the rhythmic clapping of a horse's hooves.

CXVIII.

"Out of the forest stepped a kindly chestnut mare, saddled
and ready for her master. She inched up beside the knight
with muzzling affection as be brought forth half a carrot
from his waist bag. Then with slow precision he mounted her.
Daphne was aghast. 'Out of nothing you produce a horse!'
'Actually,' he rejoined, 'I left her where I found you,
and she came through the forest to meet us. And now, adieu.'

CXIX.

"Confounded and confused, Daphne could barely cry out, 'Wait!
If she knows her way through the forest, why did we not ride?'
He answered with a calm, assuring tone. 'In these cases,
it's better that a person find her own way, as you did.'
'But why did you walk all those dusty miles with me?' she asked.
'We had things to talk about. I'm sure as you remember,
you will understand.' On these words, he turned and departed.

CXX.

"Churning inside but wasting no time in bewilderment,
she also turned, and before the forest could swallow the knight,
she was marching back up the path to find the cut, the means
of her ascent. Coming upon what looked to be a crease
in the curtain of time, she summoned herself and began
her climb, moving briskly left then right, but ever up, up,
finding footholds and handles her mere eyes could not discern.

CXXI.

"The jagged rocks nicked and cut her bare legs and scraped her hands,
and the bold exertion clutched her breath, but still she mounted,
moving in a zone of no thought, by present purpose held,
propelled up the rock face that proved unworthy as a foe.
She scaled the entire height in a relentless quarter hour,
and spent another quarter standing on the high summit,
self-aware, triumphant, and far beyond all weight of pride.

CXXII.

"It was then she saw the city, as if coalescing
into matter before her, a resplendent drapery
wrapped on the green hills descending toward a potent river.
There marble mansions with bordered terraces and gardens
dense with clustered roses of every color met the eye;
there a walkway through a piazza of majestic palms
brought one to a grand amphitheatre of polished stone.

CXXIII.

"And everywhere sculptured fountains brimming and cascading
in ordered and most joyous celebration of beauty,
verdancy and life. It was a place of distilled magic,
as if each region of the earth had offered up its best
element—a nugget or a jewel or a flower—
brought here for Heaven's masonry and artful ornament.
To see this place and know what one is seeing needs higher mind.

CXXIV.

"But who could be the residents of these most sacred hills?
What people could these be, who understood with clarity
of vision nonpareil the hidden laws of harmony?
Without these wordy thoughts but blessed understanding high,
Daphne gazed at what was before her till she herself filled
with that same clarity and knew her purpose and took it
as a spouse. Only then came her first descending step.

CXXV.

"She spied a road exiting the thick forest and winding
toward the gate of this exquisite place, but there was no path
going down the hill. The earth crumbled under the pressure
of her steps, each foothold disintegrating as she took
the next. Barely avoiding a headlong tumble, she made
the bottom and the road, the part of her that could not know
the height she'd been to glad to stand on habitual ground.

CXXVI.

"No sooner had she reached the road and turned toward city gate
when from behind she heard hard familiar comic clopping.
'The knight!' she declaimed, and turned to face the crippled rider
who, now nearly upon her, hailed her with a friendly wave.
'I thought you said you were going home,' she said, limp fatigue
dampening her accusation. 'Ah, but I am,' he said.
'Climb aboard. I'll take you to our city and find your work.'

CXXVII.

"'Our city!' she exclaimed. 'If only I had known, Sir Knight,
I would have ridden our horse to get here. How easily
I forget what is mine. Tell me, what else belongs to me?'
The knight replied in gentle, fatherly admonition.
'Now Daphne, I'm sure you see there was no place for a horse
on your hilltop. Not always is there an easier way,
and to think there should be is to put a tax on Heaven.'

CXXVIII.

"'Now climb.' He extended his hand and with surprising ease
in one graceful turn lifted her to her place behind him.
The horse moved deliberately, and soon the city gates
appeared, well wrought in stone and iron, but not magnificent;
rather covered in flowering plants and flanked by great palms,
more a portal of hope than a defense. Seeing the knight,
the gatekeeper smiled broadly and the gates spread in welcome.

CXXIX.

"They moved as if on tour along the road shaded by palms
of all kinds and decorated by roses and citrus.
Three quarters round a roundabout in whose ivied center
stood an elegant gilded goddess on marble column,
they turned up a kindred road toward a focal edifice,
a grand villa, not sumptuous or proud like a palace,
but central, classical, restrained and sweet in symmetry.

CXXX.

"Around it like perfect draperies spread ordered gardens
of all kinds: palms and shade trees in stately geometry,
at their feet green grass and tulips of every color,
roses spaced by category and abundant arbors,
citrus, banana, trellises of flowering vines, songbirds,
aromatic herbs surrounding ancient olive trees,
even a broad arc of vegetables in grand array.

CXXXI.

"Within these gardens, in placements pleasing, were to be found
fountains small and large, bubbling forth soothing sounds round statues
of cheerful cherubs or serene water-bearing ladies,
or jetting out their celebration round the high figures
of great gods, mythic immortals. Never had Daphne seen
a place so plentifully watered, nor water better
used for beauty and the summoning of best attention.

CXXXII.

"As the horse, disciplined to mild service, strode dutifully,
its riders—the wise, watchful male calmly undistracted
and the flowering female delighted by new beauty—
shared silently their sweetened awareness of these gardens,
each other, and themselves therein. Each worker that they passed
raised an eye of benign greeting, a smile, a nod, a wave.
In an overflowing state, they reached the central villa.

CXXXIII.

"Dismounting carefully, the steadfast knight brought Daphne down
as if weightless and ushered her through the villa's side door
where she found herself in a kitchen's bright activity.
Shoulder to shoulder were cooks before huge grills tending meat,
while back to back with them were others stirring sauces, soups
and vegetable concoctions. To their left and right, others
kneaded bread dough or fixed details on delicate desserts.

CXXXIV.

"Past the chef, cooks and plate preparers were a row of sinks
where stood a line of cheerful friends washing and polishing
the china and crystal. There the knight led Daphne, awestruck
at this human beehive of merry work. Tapping the arm
of a lady at a sink, he whispered a brief message;
she quickly removed her gloves and apron and left her place
which he with open hand invited Daphne to approach.

CXXXV.

"At first confused, Daphne felt her stomach trip in surprise
as she realized what was being asked of her. She held
herself still and issued an impulsive questioning cry.
'All this way to wash dishes? Is this how I know the good?'
Only a tiny few workers missed a moment disturbed
at her mournful whine; benevolent smiles upturned the lips
of many more. The knight gestured again, and he too smiled.

CXXXVI.

"Answering something higher than a chafed sense of justice,
Daphne moved to the sink, donned the apron and gloves and took
her place in the work. The first few plates she swabbed less with poise
than with self-pity, but abandoning that emotion
by repeated effort she brought herself to see and touch
each dish she cleaned bright. Though she knew not its name, acceptance
came to her, and on its heels she discovered moving rest.

CXXXVII.

"Some minutes in her task, she felt the gentlest bodiless push,
as if of fine air, on the crown of her head, directing
her gaze down into the sink. There on the topmost dish looked
in reflection her own face, or was it hers? Radiant,
beatific in color, calm and clarity—her, yes,
as if pure soul. Her gasp erased the vision. Echoed
a thought, 'Be not shocked at the opening of Heaven's door.'

CXXXVIII.

There Mathilde stopped, her own face and those of us around her
radiant as Daphne's in the dish. Breath moved easily,
and a sweet silence ensued. Our loving configuration,
unhidden but invisible in the noisy airport,
for some moments became a crown of seven self-points sure
of higher touch. The hubbub of human travel, its loud
surging wasteful complexity, found no door to intrude.

CXXXIX.

At last Mathilde resumed. "As I told you, the precise point
at which I drifted and the tale became my dream is not
for measure, but if you've heard the end of the tale, the dream
continued, to one surpassing episode. There I was,
myself not Daphne, standing at the edge of the city,
looking through the gate at the looming world of earthly sense
which surrounded and threatened to devour the sacred place.

CXL.

"Then just outside the open gate appeared a frightful form,
a screaming woman with a strident face, my own mother—
though not the prudent parent that I knew; rather she stood
as an angry goddess—taller, tense, certain of her claim.
With bloodshot eyes, she brayed of duty and danger and death.
'Return at once!' Behind her, past the edge of clarity,
stood my father, but faceless, a dark prince of cruelty.

CXLI.

"My grandmere had her hand on the device that moved the gate,
which, it was clear, she could not close without assent from me.
Her face was lit with an accepting love, but paralyzed;
she owned no will in this but waited to respond to mine.
Behind me, within the gate, as far back as my father
stood before me, the knight attended all, without shirking
or hoping, his just comprehension unperturbed and clear.

CXLII.

"A resolution waited on my choice, but as I watched,
watching became more difficult. The screaming virago
made herself more audible, more visceral, more possessed
and more possessing, and her puppeteer would soon make her
too real to resist. No choice from me, no active movement
to maintain my state was all they needed to reclaim me,
pull me back outside the gate to their enveloping lies.

CXLIII.

"I blew a kiss to my grandmere whose face remained unchanged
but whose hand made the move to close the gate. She took her place
outside, bold in front, defying with her radiant eyes
the desperate rabid screaming of the mad mock mother
whose noise shrank to sibilant idiocy and puffed out.
The dark prince posed dire and implacable, no doubt planning
new strikes, even as his form fell indistinct and faded.

CXLIV.

"Now more aware of my attention, I turned to the knight
and saw him face to face whose face was truth and moved to him
not in supplication but in new knowledge of myself.
Our extended hands met and joined. There is no more for words."
Mathilde was silent. Soon the place where we all were waiting
surrounded us again; again the noisy grind of time
grew up, around and within, to claim what it owned of us.

End, Book One

Book Two: *A Prince for the Pea Princess*

I.

A thunderclap so strong the building shook disturbed the crowd,
and audible vibration from the windows and the roof
greeted the gasps of those who had been dozing. Soon followed
lightening, not intermittent flickering but a huge burst,
bold and sustained, illuminating the rutted stresses
of resignation in the faces all around. Jules smiled,
"Dear friends, that was like the flash from a cosmic photograph."

II.

"Good thought," Anamusa avowed. "How illuminating
it is to be the object of the dear Gods' attention."
"I'm still savoring Mathilde's sweet story," Carroll offered,
"but I'll need a drink to cleanse my palate before the next."
"Most of us just listen to stories, Carroll, not eat them,"
Marco giggled, then added, "I'm not mocking you, good friend,
just noting our dependence on the metaphorical."

III.

"I understand, " said Carroll. "Even my low wattage bulb
still throws a little light." Marco nodded knowingly.
"What choice have we who would use language," sighed Jules as he smiled,
"but to discuss what the world's like instead of what it is?"
"I'm getting lost," worried Ruby. "Precisely my point.
You're not actually lost," continued Jules, "but your words
liken confusion to not knowing where you are. You see?"

IV.

"I do see," Ruby quipped, "and hear and taste and touch and smell,
but I'm not sure I understand." Mathilde admonished all,
"Let the wit be suspended before it has descended."
"Yes, let's all cleanse our palates, so to speak," Jules suggested,
'and when we sit down again, I'll take my turn and tell you
a tale modeled on the work of Hans Christian Andersen,
an homage to the master who kept my youth from drowning."

V.

"And yet another metaphor," chided Anamusa,
but the group, already stirring and standing, had the sense
to let the matter dissolve in the air, making their way
to refreshment and brief relief. The teeming terminal
had grown tired; a slouched and drooping multitude filled the chairs,
as if poured and now congealing, shifting in lumps, snoring.
Ah, I too fall into metaphors. The mind is language.

VI.

Having reassembled, we loyal friends prepared ourselves
for listening: an active, self-aware attending work
done in respect, in calm, with special effort to avoid
rude interrupting, whether spoken or silent in the throat.
For what worth can it be to pose polite in listening
while loose internal chattering crowds and closes the brain?
In poised postures of readiness, we awaited Jules' words.

VII.

He began, "I hope that I have made it clear already
how much the tales of Master Andersen guided the growth
of my budding soul. I was a child often unhappy,
given to vain self-pity, though I suffered so much less
than those around me. My native city, Bucharest, choked
in the grip of a sick dictator. Many barely ate;
all longed for light and knew the pangs of empty helplessness.

VIII.

"But I was lucky, as all of us here have always been.
My father was an educated man, a professor
at the dental college, who, though suffering poor wages
and professional indignity, managed to keep
through my entire youth the job that kept his family whole.
He did so by loving his students, cherishing his friends
and remaining dead silent about the government's crimes.

IX.

"So easy it is to condemn the silent compliance
of prisoners, to call them cowards, self-deceiving sheep.
I know better. My father did not look for justice here
on earth, nor did he curse God. He relied on reasoning.
Deeply had he plumbed the question of human suffering
and had concluded there must be an economy there,
a provision for an unfathomable higher world.

X.

"Further than that vague, sustaining stopping point, he ventured
blindly, ineffectively, never permitting himself
to glimpse the next dimension, never understanding those
whose words beckoned from beyond. From Jesus, Moses, Buddha,
he knew only moral teaching: he had no ears to hear.
After a glass of ordinary wine, he'd often say,
'Hope's the bait I always take, my deadly idiocy.'

XI.

"By fate's decree, it was not in him to be otherwise.
He was what he was. His fundamental passive nature
gave birth to few rebellious thoughts, and the possible good
in every wound came to his mending heart too easily.
He endured, kept quiet, and his family ate, stayed warm
in winter, had a used piano and too many books.
Among those books was one that magnetized and quickened me.

XII.

"My mother had brought to the marriage an old translation
of selected tales of Andersen; by whom selected
I never knew, but Heaven must have approved the choices,
for these two dozen short stories nourished my begging heart
like no other food. Strangely, the translation was English,
not Romanian, as my mother as a girl had gone
to London with a gymnastics team sponsored by the state.

XIII.

"Her career as a gymnast was short, stopped by her body's
overgrowth of gangly limbs as girlhood gave way to green
womanhood. But from this once-in-her-lifetime trip—to her
a 'hiatus from hell'—she brought back three books in English.
I have them still, in my library, now bound in leather:
Shakespeare's complete plays and poems; Old Testament stories
for children, with illustrations; and the Andersen tales.

XIV.

"When still not school age, I discovered these books in our shelves.
The Shakespeare volume was set in tiny type, its pages
delicate as moth wings. To my young hands and eyes it seemed
a daunting glut of adult dealings, far beyond my grasp.
The pictures in the book of Bible stories reassured
my mind, but the long robes the figures wore were alien.
The Andersen book seemed harmless, the lightest of the three.

XV.

"Leaving Shakespeare for later life, I took the other two
to mother and in a bold declaration too bizarre
to forget—I was an undemanding child who rarely
had anything to assert—I shocked us both with these words:
'These will be our new stories, Mother. You may pick which one
to read first, but we should not wait. I'm ready for them now.'
Long years it took to understand this angel utterance.

XVI.

"With surprised parental pride, my mother drew my young eyes
to the print on the pages. 'This is not our language, Jules.
It is English, the language spoken in America
and in England, where I bought these books. I've studied English
only on my own in private not in school, learning it
with a heart of secret hope but no teacher to help me.
To read these books is to be blind in a field together.'

XVII.

"But there was never really any question we would try,
find some way. We both sensed something living in this labor:
for her, the effort was a legacy of heart treasure
and trust; for me, a growth of mind, an expensive purchase
bought with more pure attention than I'd ever had to pay.
She would read the English roughly, in stiff, scarred syllables,
stopping every other sentence to translate as she could.

XVIII.

"My ears grew used to English in my mother's toiling voice.
It was like grain stored in a granary for future use,
and in the famine of my adolescence, when the chance
to learn the language more by study came my way, I felt
the rhythms of her voice, stored in memory, brace my mind's
travel through the shafts of alien sounds. Her translations—
awkward, halting, fanciful, bland—were a kind of longing.

XIX.

"And so I first was given the Bible, this strange domain
of stiff-necked folk struggling for and against their God.
It was grave and weighty to me, even in the dilute
children's version we were using. I did not resent it,
but listening to it was like hoisting something heavy
again and again. One grows muscles fit for adult work
under the sun in an arid land of olden glory.

XX.

"Of course I did not know what I was hearing—wandering,
war and wonder. Over months we dutifully followed
the patriarchs from Sumer down to Egypt, through Moses'
fearsome miracles and the making of the Holy Ark.
It was not children's business, yet children still should know it.
I quickened to the frogs, the killing angel, the drowned chariots,
shattered tablets, food from Heaven—life as sacred conflict.

XXI.

"Taking it in brought accelerated furrowing
of the brow of childhood. Finally there came a young man,
David, whose crazy bravery thrilled me. Him I could touch
at my mind's most mature edge. In him I could imagine
myself, standing before a huge horror, ready to die—
whatever dying was—defending the great God's honor.
But breathing this young hero's air, I hoped we'd done enough.

XXII.

"Mother understood, laid aside these stories, and took up,
without a rest, the other volume. I girded myself
for mental battle once again, but what came was not war.
With Andersen's first tale, 'The Princess and the Pea', I learned
a new state, thoughtful delight, which grew with each new story.
Listening to this man—my mind addressed, my heart engaged—
I was more fully myself than I'd ever been before.

XXIII.

Jules paused to punctuate his claim and collect himself,
but the space was quickly filled by the shock of Ruby's name:
'…West Coast Airlines passenger Ruby Dareling, please come
to the customer service desk.' The request repeated.
She stood, excused herself, and while we waited briskly walked
the stretch of checkerboard tiles to a uniformed lady,
chatted briefly to her, and returned among us, informed.

XXIV.

"It is as we assumed: that this rough weather won't abate
until near dawn, that every room in easy taxi reach
is filled, that tickets will be honored on tomorrow's flights
as space permits, and that small blankets are available.
Tomorrow we're to get a complimentary boxed meal."
Jules mused, "The creature comforts soothing this inclemency
are more than we need, together and happy as we are."

XXV.

"Why did they page you, Ruby?" wondered Carroll. "Had you
inquired at our last brief break?" Ruby replied, "Yes, I found
myself transported by Mathilde's tale, but then the sharp thought
stung me that I may've missed some news about rescheduled flights."
"That's the danger of stories," Carroll warned. "They pull the mind
so deeply in, so captivate attention, we neglect
the wider world. What a wondrous work true listening is!"

XXVI.

"True, Carroll," Ruby concurred, "yet even as I waited
at the desk to hear the news, something in me realized
there was none, that one of us would've heard it and told the rest."
"We pay the ransom of each other's sleep," Carroll affirmed,
"and together make clarity of each one's confusion.
But conceive of a man who drifts not in and out, himself
and the world never unobserved." "We know that man," said Jules.

XXVII.

His comment introduced a silent space wherein each one
renewed his double grip, and, aware of his attention,
felt the gratitude of traveling with those of like mind.
Jules seemed in no rush to resume his tale, and so Mathilde,
looking to her right beyond my head, saluted Carroll.
"I'm thinking now how similar were features of my tale
to those of Lewis Carroll; I intended no trespass."

XXVIII.

She went on, "I know you honor him, even taking
his last name to be your first. I hope you'd not intended
a story in his style as your offering to our game."
His reply rode not on a cursory grin, but a broad,
relaxed and lasting smile, welling up from deep within him,
called to the surface by her sweet concern. "Far more distinct
than similar was your tale. You've taken nothing from me."

XXIX.

"So you already know your story?" Ruby asked, alarm
tainting her voice. "I don't know what I'm doing in this game.
I have no story all prepared and doubt there's one to find
in the storage of my brain. I'm standing empty-handed
at the gift table. Is mine the only unconcocted
contribution here?" She caught herself and sighed. "Excuse me.
Worry over worthiness—the old story of my life."

XXX.

At this Anamusa cast a probing glance at Marco
who nodded in return and spoke. "Ana and I may work
together on our stories, Ruby. We have agreement
but no plan. And I'm sure you read too much in Carroll's words."
"Yes," said Carroll, "I only meant to reassure Mathilde.
I promise you, there are no plots among us." Jules giggled
and affirmed, "I'm not even sure how my own tale will end."

XXXI.

Even I felt pulled to offer Ruby something soothing.
"I haven't the foggiest notion what Heaven will put
in my head. I'm just glad I can see there's nothing there now."
All turned in my direction, and I witnessed their efforts
not to burst into laughter. Barely containing myself—
the silliness of my own words echoing in my ears—
I asked, "Jules, are you ready to resume? I do hope so."

XXXII.

A kind smile lit Jules' face from mouth to eyes as if the sun
were chasing off the morning shadow from a bedroom porch.
"I was discussing my discovery of Andersen.
I'd like to be precise describing the effect he had,
for I think he, perhaps like no one else I've ever read,
summons me to the peak of the parapet, the highest
step of word and thought, past which is only conscious being."

XXXIII.

"We all know that state," said Anamusa. "Each day anew
begins our slow climb to reach it and then take off in flight,
sweet prolonged soaring, until we lose the uplifting air
and earth intrudes to snatch us back." "And then again we climb,"
said Marco with no pause. "So have our lives become, " said Jules,
"and for that reason I'd suggest our first experience
with that state is a milestone, a true sacrament for each."

XXXIV.

"And as with you and Andersen, so each of us can tell
of his first ascent of essence mind answering the call
of higher consciousness. 'In the beginning was the word,'
beckoning us beyond words." "Yes, Carroll," Jules continued,
"and if not a written word, perhaps a painted image
of a face in bliss or a mist rising above mountains.
Our first visit to Heaven's porch defines the rest of life."

XXXV.

"Even I have such a moment. At least I think I do."
All turned to face Ruby, gladdened by her self-inclusion.
"Please tell us, Ruby," Marco said, now suddenly aware,
as were all, that she had finally offered us the chance
to love her by our listening. She began haltingly.
"I don't know if this is right, especially as Jules talks
about his great moment coming in his childhood. Not mine."

XXXVI.

"O but tell us, " Jules said with reassuring eagerness.
"My childhood was not a childhood. It was a fight for life,
a war for survival. The moment we've been talking of
did not come for me until much later, in my twenties,
during the first pure vacation of my life." Ruby paused.
"Where were you?" Anamusa asked, not wanting to let her
stop for long. "Yes, Ana, that's the strange part—where I was. Rome.

XXXVII.

"By then I'd been in—the Army I mean—about nine years.
I was stationed in Germany and had some leave, two weeks,
so my friend Audrey and I decided to go see Rome.
Can you imagine—two black American soldier girls
on a Roman holiday? From the train station we took
a cab. I remember the Rome traffic was appalling,
Audrey was hungry, and we rode without destination.

XXXVIII.

"For ten minutes we argued on what to tell the driver.
'First food,' Audrey kept proclaiming. Finally he gave up,
pulled over and pointed to the meter. But where were we?
'Villa Bourghese.' And what was that? Again he pointed.
We decided to get out and try again, but something
in me fancied it was fate to explore this foreign place.
Hungry Audrey grudgingly agreed to give me an hour.

XXXIX.

"To keep it short, I was overwhelmed. Never in my life
had I been in an art museum. It took half an hour
just to slow down and let the pieces work on my senses.
The statue of Apollo and the girl running from him
finally stopped me and made me really look. Then I went
upstairs, turned left into a gallery and confronted
my life arrested before me in a shocking instant.

XL.

"There was David, holding the head of Goliath, the sword
with which he'd done his task drooping in his right hand, his face
a tense mixture of accomplishment and sorrow and disgust.
His stomach could not quite hold down the warrior fate he saw.
That was my moment—wordless, perfect, true—though I shuddered
and wanted not to look. O, Caravaggio, you knew!
There and then something began its slow growth. And here I am."

XLI.

"Remarkable!" said Marco. "Nothing less," Carroll added.
A moment of silence ensued, after which Jules whispered,
"Bravo, Ruby, and thank you." Anamusa turned to Jules,
"So will you now finish your framing story? I believe
Andersen had just taken you where Caravaggio
took Ruby, and where all of us began our waking quest,
that moment of self-knowledge that starts the pearl. Please go on."

XLII.

"Yes, please do," urged Marco. "I hope we haven't robbed you, Jules.
It seems your framing tale divided itself and became
a discussion." "Perhaps it's best," Mathilde consoled, "for now
all understand the point a framing story would have made.
We've composed the overture rather than listened to it."
"I suppose you can go right to your tale, Jules," Marco said.
An Andersen sequel of some kind, was it not, my friend?"

XLIII.

Quickly Jules picked up the thread. "I had thought to offer you
a sequel to 'The Toad', a poignant and beautiful tale
of earthly lowliness, humility and innocence
that ends in spiritual triumph; but I realized
I was projecting myself into the story, wanting
it to be my own life I was narrating. Andersen
deserves better service than my sentimentality.

XLIV.

"So instead I'm set to try a tale I'm not sure about;
that is, I don't know how it will end. The resolution
of a tale is the best measure of the author's being.
If this telling flies, then Mathilde's astounding offering
will have a fit companion piece. If it sinks, the challenge
of a problem I don't yet understand is my reward
for trying. There are no losers in a game among friends."

XLV.

Jules cleared his throat and shifted in the plastic airport chair,
taking on a posture more erect, but calm, tensionless—
or so it seemed—and when he spoke it was no longer Jules
but an older man of regal quality, with a voice
as smooth and slowly certain in its syllables as love
is certain, flowing on in true untroubled clarity.
"My story may be useful to good souls who'd marry well.

XLVI.

"As you know from Angel Andersen's sweet but brief account,
far as my most remote ideas sent me—not so far
by standards of today—I'd searched for a bride, a helpmate,
an ally with the feminine grace required to balance
and complement the constancy to which my soul aspired.
As I would be unbending, she would be all merciful.
As firm as my unchanging gaze, so bright would be her smile.

XLVII.

"My search had failed because in my blunt youth I knew not then
one searches vainly for a prize one is not ready for.
I did not know myself, and so my urgency to find
a mate was misdirected; my thoughts of what I wanted
were distorted. In youth abundant thrust kicks up the sand
and wraps us in a cloud that only Gods can penetrate.
My heart was not wrong, but a horse needs a clear-eyed rider.

XLVIII.

"And so from one long foray out I had returned, as fall
advanced in sorrow and the rains, not harsh or hateful yet,
slowly surrendered themselves from the sky's pent up lament.
I was disconsolate and very, very tired. My horse
had trudged the last few miles with drooping head unpiloted,
footsore, seeking only warm straw and food's forgetfulness.
The fire in my chambers dried my clothes, not my drowning heart.

XLIX.

"Mystery and misery, for man you are close siblings!
What was my wrong? How was my true vision vexed and tainted,
that among so many daughters of the neighboring kings
I could not find the princess I so longed for? Nothing clear
rooted my objections, but every girl—some of great wealth,
many of fair refinement, all by regal duty raised—
every girl dissatisfied me. Was I to be a monk?

L.

"In every castle, in every interview, I'd waited
for the rush of elevation, the firm sign from within,
but it had not come, and there I sat, making drab small talk
in palaces, waiting out the time one gives to dead hope.
By the last few stops, mine was a memorized embassy,
a rote display of manners. My focus had descended
to the food. Soul lost to sweet tastes, I had become my horse.

LI.

"Then for a week I sat in chambers, a gloom factory,
condensing moist self-pity from the very air. The clouds
confirmed my joyless homecoming, gathering, thickening,
their dark accumulations longing to pour forth on all
the lonely unwed landscape my small window afforded
to my eye. Was this the will of Heaven, that I remain
alone, unpartnered, solely to myself? So be it, Lord.

LII.

"And from my grief began to grow the muscle of resolve.
What does it mean to be a solitary and true prince?
I was not friendless, not starved in isolation. To me
a steward, an architect and a court philosopher
loyally reported. Even the gaunt court physician,
who saw the task of keeping my body in right function
as the only real work, deigned to converse on occasion.

LIII.

"And there were numbered others—cooks and tutors, acrobats,
comedians, scribes and dull-faced laborers—there to keep
me company. If the hierarchy of nobility
demanded that I never be their chummy fellow—
just as Heaven limited its intimacy with me—
I still had something. I could look down or up. The longing
for true partnership, only that remained to scrape my breast.

LIV.

"As clouds must do, however dark and thick, my clouds poured forth
and then dispersed, leaving a crystal sky which called me out,
out of my throes, out of my room, out to some worthy work.
I descended the stair humming, springing to a rhythm
frisky and buoyant, rising in readiness to attend
the new day's challenge. But upon entering the great hall,
I found my ancient father, furrow-faced, weakly pacing.

LV.

"'Ah, there you are,' he said, his eyes dark pools of woe, not spilled
but to their brim. 'We wondered if and when you would appear.
The storm last night was great. You must have seen it gathering.
There is damage to the roof, and the branches littering
the courtyard and the gardens will require a dozen men
a dozen days of clearing, but to that work I'm equal.
To the other prodigy the storm produced, I bow down.'

LVI.

"For a moment I had no breath and not a germ of thought.
The king's distress was wrenching, and his age so visible.
'What trouble is this, dear father?' I managed to utter.
'Why the girl at the gate,' he replied, stifling a lament.
'Her claim and her appearance so belie each other, boy,
that no normal mind can hold them both at once. Confusion
has the throne this morning, and age surrenders to the coup.'

LVII.

"He stayed silent for more heartbeats than my bold youth could bear.
'What's to be done?' finally I faintly asked, all baffled.
My father sighed deeply as if dying. 'It's in the Queen's hands,
hers and our physician's. They're already at work on it.
They never rest, that meddling pair, but now they've got a job
that will task their clever powers of dark conspiracy;
that is, if this girl is the princess that she says she is.'

LVIII.

"'Princess!' I started and shook inside as if the ground quaked.
'Aye, that's the claim she brings from out of nowhere, standing drenched
at our gate in darkest night, no shame in her beseeching
our best hospitality. To all questions she replies,
'All that in time; now here I am for your kind attention.'
'I couldn't refuse her, even noted a pinch of joy
at serving her, despite the queen's most blatant scowls and snarls.'

LIX.

"'So we know nothing of her but her being here?' I asked.
'That's it. All else must wait till she descends, ready, I hope,
to loosen the mystery. Meanwhile the queen rampages,
fearing being undermined again at choosing your bride.'
'Again?' said I. 'Why, yes. When you departed on your search,
she was dispossessed in dread. Your return without a bride
delighted her. She has designs on you and on the realm.'

LX.

"'Whole architectures, no doubt,' I said, 'founded on theories
that only she can understand. But what of the princess?'
'As I say, she's above, assuming she's survived the test
of the queen's dire accommodations. 'Survived? You don't think...?'
'With that poisonous physician whispering in her ear,
I put nothing past her. I am too old, too enfeebled
to resist her. This is your fate and fight. Beware, my boy.'

LXI.

"With that he turned, a well draped drooping skeleton leading
in surrender his faded spirit to its final prayers.
Hardly had the exhausted king retired when the queen lurched
down the corridor in frigid stridency, her shrill voice
a nail on slate. 'Certainly by now the rude imposter
has awakened. Where is she? Bring her forth!' Then seeing me
standing in the hall, she bit off a smile of cold command.

LXII.

"'Ah! Has our young scion really left his sanctuary?
Could the threat the realm is under have pricked his cold conscience?
I doubt it. I bet it's simple happenstance that graces
us with his jiggly and naïve attention.' This she snarled
as if to an unseen jury as she strode down the hall.
Without looking back she barked, 'Come, boy. Our dear physician
waits already stationed, attending at the door of fraud.'

LXIII.

"I followed down the corridor which echoed the queen's fanged
rhetoric until we reached the smallest, most distant room
that could house a human. There the physician stood ready,
his eyebrows as if permanently arched, focused firmly
on the handle of the door. 'Open it!' bellowed the queen.
A servant jumped, the door was opened, and there stood a hill
of piled bedding against which leaned the realm's tallest ladder.

LXIV.

"'Up and rouse the girl!' A younger servant sprang up the rungs,
but before he'd climbed a third the height, a voice from atop
the mountain of mattresses, as if from Heaven itself,
arrested all movement, even our breathing. 'Stop all this!'
it said, faintly but with a tone of silken certainty.
'I am not asleep, now or have I been. Who can sleep here,
unwelcome on this feathered cliff of hospitality?'

LXV.

"I loved her before I saw her face. 'I am coming down.
No help, please.' Step by cautious step, a form descended.
All but the queen looked away in modesty as the skirts
of the self-knowing princess fluttered out from her legs.
Three full minutes were absorbed in her self-presentation;
we waited, awkwardly aware, unable to divert
our attention, unable to go further in our minds.

LXVI.

"After setting one foot and then—so intentionally—
the other down, she turned her mysterious smile on us.
The corners of her mouth seemed suggestively uplifted,
not by any muscle stress, but by a light and lightness,
a radiance that emanated from her to create
and fill the present, give it space and body, let it see
and speak. In gazing at her, I never felt more myself.

LXVII.

"Her physical form was just, though not what one remembered.
No poor proportions, rude extremes, no stamp of closed culture—
nothing to cavil in her flesh or hair or height or girth.
Focusing past the queen and the physician, who stood close
as their clothes would let them, she found me, and in that instant
a circuit of clarity arched between us, and the rest
of life and labor, rule and service, shrank to simple task.

LXVIII.

"The queen rumbled as to speak, but I intercepted her
and shocked myself and all about with the authority
of my words. The princess, I declared, would move herself in
to my own quarters and reside there while I was away.
She would receive every gracious attention due to her,
the whole house stand in service. I would be leaving shortly.
On all other matters, I ordered, await my return.

LXIX.

"The queen's mouth gaped. The physician stared. Even the princess
issued an eighth note of surprise in the lighted music
of her eyes. I raised my hand to interrupt and arrest
a thought that flashed on the queen's face before it became speech.
 'No more,' I said. 'I will be master here soon, soon enough.
The king my father will confirm all that I've here ordained.
I'll speak to him before I leave. You all know your places.'

LXX.

"I turned my eyes to the princess, she to mine. In our gaze,
we drank a solemn toast of understanding and offered
silently a perfect loyalty, one to the other.
I bowed to end our speechless interview and down the hall
moved in heedful haste to my father's chapel, finding him
on his knees, muttering exhausted, well-intentioned prayers.
'My father, I've come to inform you of my rising aims.'

LXXI.

"'Still on his knees, he turned to me, recognition slowly
reforming his countenance. 'I'd given up hope,' he said.
'How this sudden change?' 'When I saw her, I knew my princess.
What follows will issue from a higher intelligence.
In faith, I only know that I must go as directed
and some completing trial will present itself to me.
Till I return, you must hold out. Steel yourself in command.'

LXXII.

"'The queen would cast her out to be forgotten.' 'Worse,' I said.
'She and her physician would be masters here and will stop
at nothing. They would destroy her, as you've already warned.
Protect her till my return though you yourself are threatened.'
'I am weak with age; I strain to walk, but I've learned some tricks
through the years. Do as your source directs, but do not tarry.'
"I left him standing, eyes up, rallied to a last challenge.""

LXXIII.

"I ordered not my horse, but a wagon and team of four
loaded with a yard of the flower garden's richest loam.
It seemed most strange, but the instant knowing that informed me
came unbidden and by explaining would be chased away.
Suffice to say I set out with few provisions, no set
directions, a weighty burden of soil, a task unknown—
but from the God in me a calm electric certainty.

LXXIV.

"By the time the gates closed behind me, the noon sun held sway
in the sky, and its warm radiance dried the humid air.
I set out west. Was I to complete the circuit begun
in the east by my father's forebears and followed in faith
by uncounted generations? Sought I the western sea
and the vantage of a naked pinnacle from which time
would not exist, devoured by the great expanse of ocean?

LXXV.

"The long ride took me first through hilly forests, and the team
cooperated crisply, refreshed by piney breezes,
aware of a general slow descent that made the work
of each hill a promise of a longer ease. Confidence
presided; the lone obstacle was a spoiled tedium
that every few miles blew in like an ugly grey cloudbank
to interpose itself. Remembrance of God banished it.

LXXVI.

"Coming down the last hill, a fertile valley, vast and full
of open promise that a thousand projects could not fill
draped itself before me. Here was room for high history,
for the Muses to dance and sing centuries of poems.
Here was enough for man to husband forth bounty, to found
complex cities that indulged his mind and, fulfilled below,
to forsake and forget hard won footholds on craggy scapes.

LXXVII.

"I dared not rest here, but here was happiness for horses,
and they slowed to a grudging trudge, tempted to inaction
by the meadows of green and gold grass. Men love their animals
and would indulge them, letting slack the reins and descending
from the driver's seat to sit with them in shade on soft ground.
I felt that urge, a somnolence, a loosened jaw and droop
of eyelid downward, a mind drifting into honeyed sleep.

LXXVIII.

"I sensed the mental quicksand just before a fatal grip
had taken hold, and wanting some small appropriate pain
to reinvigorate my purpose, I raised myself up
from my seat by some mere inches into an awkward crouch
sustained by muscles rarely used, and with the reins as nerves
made clear my unrelenting will. The team at first demurred,
but when the strongest mover moved, in sequence all complied.

LXXIX.

"Onward cross this fecund valley I drove, no small distance,
and every mile made unroutine by voluntary shifts
of posture and of pace. It seemed not near December here
but still-warm golden summer. When the coastal range at last
appeared, first as a vague haze above the flat horizon,
then more distinctly as an upraised rolling obstacle,
my will had a clear target and my urgency recharged.

LXXX.

"But having let me glimpse the goal, the daylight dimmed to dusk,
and I was left to find a shelter from oncoming night.
A grove of ancient gnarled oaks presented a canopy,
and there I steered and entered, guest in a dim cathedral.
Hastily I gathered wood and lit my fire. The night passed
restlessly, troubled by the sounds and shadows that arise
from dark to lead the mind astray in mad, misspent alarm.

LXXXI.

"The dawn had only to suggest itself to put me back
on the road, the horses sluggish, too sleepy to object.
The new sun lit the coastal range, a clear ascending line
from left to right, south to north, across my field of vision.
Keeping steady pressure on, I steered toward the greater heights.
By noon – and never had I earned the noon more worthily—
the massive mountain impasse imposed itself before me.

LXXXII.

"Impenetrable it seemed, but to the humble logic
of climbing step by step. Within another steadfast hour,
I gazed upon a pathless scale where horses could not help.
My will was naked to the jagged rock. I led the beasts
to shade beneath a sharp outcrop, unharnessed them to let
them graze, loosely tethered to each other and the wagon.
Then I set off to see what God allows a man to see.

LXXXIII.

"For half an hour, the rocky slope was steep but walkable.
By leaning so far forward that my forehead kissed a knee
with every stride, I labored up and up, counting each breath.
But then the steady incline ended as the mountain arched
its granite back and snowy neck—full upright assertion
of its pitiless dominance—halting my naïve quest.
My thoughts strained to the top but tumbled back down upon me.

LXXXIV.

"From my departure all the way across the warm valley
and up to this hard-won height, I had progressed without plan,
driven by the wordless understanding, the crystalline
necessity engendered by the gaze of the princess.
But before this last, near vertical demand, I slackened
and drooped, despaired of reaching the pinnacle. Attempting
to remember God only affirmed my own nothingness.

LXXXV.

"I die here, I thought. I had no answer, no idea
how to proceed. I saw no closer ledge, felt no foothold,
and silent Heaven seemed empty of interested angels.
Lone and stopped I stood, stuck in time and marked by useless thought.
The best in me held out for no retreat, no tired return
to the queen's cackling command; the worst wanted but to weep.
All but defeated, I welcomed enveloping darkness.

LXXXVI.

"But even then a process was beginning, a new phase
resulting. Scared to self-absorption by the great mountain,
my awareness missed the greater movement going on within.
A sloughing off had started—of all false inflated hope,
of greedy expectation, of old lies, of elation,
of the useless baggage that one doesn't know one carries
like rusted trophies till the passage narrows and ascends.

LXXXVII.

"Soon I sat in darkness so thick I could not see my feet,
while within, all that I was not dissolved and dropped away.
The horrors of the night became mere sounds; the bloody teeth
that stalk through sleep found nothing terrorized to seize and slash.
I watched within as all the ugly squatters, grudges, lusts,
secret sins and fancied horrors were in parade evicted
from the vault of memory and sent to outer darkness.

LXXXVIII.

"The dawn found me rested, not from sleep, but from the sweet loss
of all that I was not, the poisoned accumulations
we part with only when confronting the merciless truth.
I looked up at my task no longer a royal scion,
heir to a throne; no longer a bold young man urged by love
to great deeds; but simply a consciousness, a thing aware
wearing a suit of skin and sinew, ready for climbing.

LXXXIX.

"And climb I did. The blank escarpment wrinkled to my will
and gave forth handholds and footprops not visible before,
though it took its angry toll in bruises, bites, bloody scrapes
and straining reaches that stretched muscles to their ripping points.
Passing angels, soaring separate spirits, saw an ant
upon a wall, gripping each moment and thrusting upward,
knowing only purchase and handclasp and the higher aim.

XC.

"When a ledge of real rest arrived, the sun was right above,
gazing down directly, snuffing out the helpless shadows.
In its uncompromising light I stood and deeply breathed,
aching everywhere and glad to ache. For what was this pain
but the herald of new being, the chance to buy oneself
back from the stone world and stand aware of all awareness?
I prayed for strength to greet with love whatever lay ahead.

XCI.

"As I turned to the rock wall to find the next clutch, I caught
sight of my foot, beside which moved the head of a serpent,
half a fist thick, surfacing from its hidden hole to take
the sun. Yet my presence did not frighten it. As I watched,
its entire length brazenly emerged and arched strike-ready.
It had come not in stealth but in rage, with finality.
The sudden confrontation seized my breath and froze my feet.

XCII.

"Snakes reign by threat. They ambush, shock, divert, derange, vanish.
But the brute thing before me now hid nothing, left nowhere
to retreat but death. From out its scabbard I slid my knife
and stooped to show the beast the blade on which the sunlight shone
with a ferocious glare. A moment of great knowing filled
and poised, then into its grim eyes I directed the gleam.
It struck and left its fangy drool on the steel and sank.

XCIII.

"My boot was instantly upon it, pressing it to the ground.
I stooped again, gripped it by the throat and held it helpless.
On that slim precarious ledge, I whirled twice three circles
and cast the creature out into the air. I thought I heard
the roar of a mountain lion in sweet celebration
echo over the heights, and an eagle, taken to flight,
swooped elegantly down to where the snake had struck the rock.

XCIV.

"I did not waste a second in self-congratulation
but recommenced my climb, perfect focus re-established,
energy redoubled. The winds that buffet highest things
threw their blustery punches at my eyes and forced the dust
into my face, but they could not distract my mind. My will
had left the earth and would not be recalled by any claim
of mountain or of flesh. I became an aim ascending.

XCV.

"I climbed till the end of daylight, till I'd made a man's peace
with climbing—four hours, five, six, till my machinery—
the muscles making motion, the thoughts begetting feelings—
became inured to the escarpment and the only self
still holding claim on truth was an observing particle
of God whose willed attention hands and feet and mind obeyed.
In this state I reached the cut ridges atop the cliff face.

XCVI.

"The brow of the mountain offered itself as a staircase,
ridges ascending to a peak, a crown still not in sight.
With only the shadows of light remaining, I moved up
till I could go no higher, and there on the rocky point,
enveloped in darkness, I stopped, though not yet relenting.
I allowed no assumption of triumph. Celebration
unaccompanied by light and true vision mocks Heaven.
I knelt to attend my prayers, certainty for now eclipsed.

XCVII.

"The soft illumination that prefigures dawn found me
ready to see again, though what I saw puzzled and shocked.
I rested not on the true peak, which rose above my head
only a few feet but across a gorge, a fatal drop,
narrow but too far to leap, a last obstacle to cross.
I raised my palms to Heaven, not needing to speak my need.
As answer, that compulsion which had brought me here resumed.

XCVIII.

"I looked about with awful clarity. There on a ledge
scaled last night in near darkness were too battered topless pines,
reduced by great age to miniature but nobly paired.
I descended to the first, shorter to the eye, and found
its patient roots with my respectful sword. Its ancient trunk
sighed in glad completion, and with all my strength I bore it
up and across the last crevasse, a bridge to the real peak.

XCIX.

"To walk across the last great gap could terrorize a man,
but my will allowed no terror and my feet felt no doubt.
One step, then another, and the next and next, keeping on:
the incline accepted, the wind's buffetings absorbed, the urge
to look behind denied utterly. That interval
has no triumph in its crossing, its glory mute and blank.
One walks on as always but more aware of parting breath.

C.

"To stand on the true peak is to be oneself, crystallized
in permanent identity before the universe.
The ground beneath one does not change, nor does the far vista
except perhaps in clarity and in relationship
to all the petty claims and charges from one's earthly life.
One gazes out from inward permanence, undisturbed self,
unique, capable of single service to Creation.

CI.

"From my foothold, as the sun began its climb behind me,
the vast Western ocean was a dense stripe of darker blue
that merged at the horizon with a dazzling rosy sky.
My gaze was a call across that ocean to awaken
from among the teeming life beyond a single hero
who would found a long, unbroken, slowly westering line
of high servants brunting the earth's and the mind's brute spinning.

CII.

"I gazed until the gleam upon the sea was a signal
of a thing begun; then I turned to face the brightening sun
and resolutely walked back across the bridge given me
by Heaven in the ancient grand design. Yet as my step
lighted on the lesser peak's snow-glazed stone, a tumbling slide
of loosened rock surrendered its dead grip, and in its fall
into the gorge took the tree, the trusted span for me alone.

CIII.

"Thence unblinking went I to its brother, severed its hold
as I had done the first, and by strenuous lowerings
down the ledges, using all the rope I'd brought and the care
of a man on whom depend his dear children unaware,
I brought it and my own bruised body down the beaten mountain.
Upright in the wagon full of richest loam I stood it,
not knowing whether it could be revived, but full of faith.

CIV.

"The sweet compulsion of my mission, now near completion,
had begun a transformation into understanding.
A true princess has a daunting bride price, calculated
not in terms of property or commerce but attainment
of a worthiness of soul's perspective, a true vision
of oneself among all things, of one's purpose and one's tasks.
Without such understanding, marriage is a wrestling match.

CV.

"Having rested long and grazed their fill, the horses wanted
exercise and gladly came back under the reins to serve.
Making our way back across the valley, what a strange sight
we made: a team of four pulling a wagon in which stood
transplanted an ancient tree, being moved to a new home
and task by the driver whose posture—resolute, erect,
without strain—balanced the bright morning sun's ascent to noon.

CVI.

"The road ahead could have been a ribbon or a river
as in gentle undulations it sought the horizon,
but the eyes were content that it was a road, and the view
stretched out before them did not need the mind's old adornment.
Birds lighted on the trees; their twitters could have been music
if the notation in the ears had occupied the heart.
Gentle hands held the reins. Time was movement round a stillness.

CVII.

"The light ascended to its apogee but could not hold,
and so began its slow decline to ignorant darkness:
like everything concerning man, a climb and a descent.
All are the same—a day, a life, a nation's centuries;
and man, nobly waiting out the lightless eras, clinging
in remembrance re-established with each breath, each great age,
each birth of higher messenger, mounts the scales of serving.

CVIII.

"Sitting vigilant beside my night fire, I realized
the need for a new name. To establish true sovereignty
on the household, I would need to return as a new man.
And for those whose world is ordered and valued by habit
and custom, a new man, claiming new authority
and setting forth new ways and purposes, must have a name
that flashes a killing sword at all the old responses.

CIX.

"But a new name was not mine to choose; it could not be plucked
from the electric maze of files and labelings that make the mind.
One enters those branches and corridors, which are nothing
but the past, in hope of finding something new and useful
to the present or the future. Impossible! Nothing
truly new can be thought. New things arrive in the present
and force the present onto us, shocking us out of thought.

CX.

"So rather than try to think of a new name, I promised
Heaven to make effort to attend whatever blessing
might be sent. With my eyes on the array of ordered stars,
I spoke aloud. 'No more am I the boy, Prince Corverus,
No more my mother's son and noble father's legacy.
I am your servant and know myself by that endeavor.
If you are pleased, make plain for me the name the world may use.'

CXI.

"The silence that ensued struck me as not without humor,
and I resolved to dear patience, charmed by the chatting fire
and calmed by the assuring tapestry of sky. At dawn
I was again moving toward home. Through the fecund valley
I drove, observing undistracted how all a poor man
might want—or believe could be—was here, offering itself
in dead fulfillment. Best not dismount to touch this rich soil.

CXII.

"The tree accompanied me. Though I could not guarantee
it would flourish in its new courtyard, the radiant life
within it touched me no less that had it issued forth
in sacred song. Straight it stood in the wagon bed, bearing
its centuries of unbent nobility. Would it die?
Would it live to be the center point of a new garden
where Heaven's elect could be brought to flowering and fruit?

CXIII.

"By midday, the valley nearly crossed, the sun had risen
to such high glory as to blanch in unremitting light
the whole landscape. The eyes begged for shade, but there was no shade.
The road had recently begun its own steady ascent
back into the rocky hills where my troubled home held out
against the resident forces that would banish the guest
of new life and hold heyday for impostership and lies.

CXIV.

"Would the king collapse? Would my new authority refute
the threat? Would my folk submit to the uncompromising,
kindly rule my bride and I required? I cast the questions
out of mind but kept in use the tension of not knowing,
as the mercilessly truthful sun held me to the road.
In the far distance by the roadside, the shape of a man
began to clarify itself from out the dazzling glare.

CXV.

"In stages to my eye resolved his colorless garments,
sturdy boots, long beard, backpack, simple cap and walking staff.
Approaching patiently, I measured him and stopped, greeting
him with welcoming look which he with benign gaze returned.
For many moments, no words broke the air, and when he spoke,
his voice was as gentle as the opening of a rose.
'I can see you don't mind being a curious vision.'

CXVI.

"To his comment my face lit in mirthful smile, as one time
in my task I had entertained a thought of how I looked,
and now with care imagining how I appeared to him,
I felt amused. 'A curious vision but a real one.'
He smiled too at my reply. 'Would you like to ride a while?'
'The sun is doing business all too well today,' he said,
'and as flying would be treacherous, riding would be fine.'

CXVII.

"He mounted the wagon and sat beside me. I resumed
my course; and after many minutes of silence as intense
as the sun, I heard myself question him, though the words came
not from my brain as they broke the air. 'Where are you going?'
'Not far,' he answered. 'When you turn east up into the hills,
I'll leave you.' It did not take much wondering how he knew
my route to realize he was a sacred visitor.

CXVIII.

"'And what is your name, friend?' I asked. 'Here I'm called Gabriel.'
Then pivoting on his seat, he turned his full gaze upon me,
'And you, what is your name?' For some time I could not reply,
but then, as before, a word sounded—'Veritas'—and hung
in the air. He replied, 'I beg your pardon. Vanitas?'
After another wondering delay, I reclaimed myself
and spoke with clarity. 'What name do you think I should have?'

CXIX.

"'Are you giving me the right to christen you, son?' he asked.
'I can give you nothing, Gabriel. Rather I submit
to your determination, and I am honored by it.'
His eyes softened, deepened into wells of understanding,
and his gaze absorbed my being. 'I note your broad shoulders
and broad brow remind me of a great friend of mine and man.
How does the name and title Prince Plato sit upon you?'

CXX.

"'It is a serious name, deserving a mature man.
Am I worthy?' His voice grew grave and slow and measured.
'By his high reasoning, so many have been introduced
to the invisible and given glimpses of the soul.
We can hardly speak of worthiness, but you are ready
for a great work of your own, and a great name answered to
can keep your mind at the right elevation, Prince Plato.'

CXXI.

"We rode on in attentive silence for another mile,
when the fork leading east and up appeared. I stopped and spoke.
'So the tree will revive?' He smiled. 'It is folly to think
of Heaven failing. Here I seem to leave you to your task.'
He stepped down and I drove on. Some seconds passed—then a flash
of white light brighter than the sun's glare lit the ringing air.
I steered right onward, savoring the gift of his visit.

CXXII.

"The road home climbed too slowly to challenge my eagerness,
but by the time I noted the wagon wheels turn over
the borders of my own estate, I'd come to readiness.
The gatekeeper celebrated my approach, opening
the ceremonial panels with his own hands, waving
his arms, then fixing himself in full, self-aware salute.
I did not descend to greet him, though my heart held him close.

CXXIII.

"The manor house teemed. Heads crowded every window, opened
now to my approach. From out the arched and vaulted doorway
poured the residents—maidservants, cooks, clerks, skilled artisans,
accountants, couriers and diplomats. Musicians played,
and up to the emerald lawns came all the sunburnt fieldmen
and the shopmen in their honest grime. Faradonias,
the steward horticulturist, extended tribute's hand.

CXXIV.

"I reached down and grasped his palm; our eyes aligned in greeting.
Then I stood on the wagon seat and spoke as the new man.
'I am now Prince Plato, a great name conferred upon me
by a great presence. But I am still and ever your friend,
and I aim to be a true master whom you can't begrudge,
whom you serve in recognition and fondness, and follow
with a shared aim and a love surpassing obedience.'

CXXV.

"Rule's first step is to establish meaning, and the symbol
of that meaning held the loyal household's wonder, standing
in the wagon, a branchless trunk requiring constant care,
the present out of which the future of this realm would grow.
I looked to Faradonias for wordless confirmation
and placed my hands on the trunk. His nod of understanding
and resolve rooted our venture, and our discrete tasks fused.

CXXVI.

"Into the house I went, to my father's chambers, a son
now more protector. I found him breathing only by prayer,
alive by conscious effort. His attention rose to me
and with all his strength, as if lifting up an offering,
he gave me his message. 'My son, the princess lives and breathes.
She dances in your room.' Here followed a tender blinking,
and his mind returned to the labor of continued breath.

CXXVII.

"I found her as he'd said, lightly dancing to the music
of her own being, undisturbed by her confinement, graced
by the unearthly certainty that sees eternity
and walks in that vision. Our gaze unto each other held
in point all that had been, all that is and all that will be.
I extended my open hand and on it rested hers;
we moved together lightly to the great hall of the house.

CXXVIII.

"Within a minute all the residents had gathered round.
With uplifted voice, I spoke. 'As my readiness to rule
permits my father to retire to his prayers and finish life
in noblest example, so my readiness to marry
beckons a new era of love. I have searched far and wide,
recognizing none among the daughters of the houses.
Now she has come to me. God's readiness has become ours.'

CXXIX.

"There rose a gentle clamor from the pressing residents.
'Let her speak to us,' they cried. 'The queen has kept her from us.'
Said Decius the obedient scholar stepping up,
'Yes, this is the first many of us have seen of her.
We knew she was here under your protection, but her face
was unknown to us, and Dr. Sinua warned against her,
that she breathed a foreign plague we were ill-equipped to bear.'

CXXX.

"'The only plague ended when she arrived,' I said smiling.
Again from the multitude, 'And what is her name? Tell us.'
At this I faltered. All I had done had been accomplished
through the instigation of her gaze, her sweet radiance.
From first seeing her, she'd never been so distant from me
as to need a name. But she perceived I had no answer
and stepped forward. The whole room hushed in solemn attendance.

CXXXI.

"'I am Princess Lumine from the land of Abovona,
not far from here, never far, but often hard to locate.'
Her voice left no echo, no resound, as if not a voice,
but her name was instantly in every mind forever,
and the riddle of her birth and birthplace still teases thought.
She stepped back and looked to me. Called to perfect clarity
by the light of her countenance, my will could not but rule.

CXXXII.

"'I now announce our wedding, and a festival of love
such as our land has never seen. Before tomorrow night,
let us transform the house into Heaven's own embassy.
Renew each surface with your scrubbing, illuminate it
with the labor of a new life's promise. Your best garments
bring forth to dress your best attention in well-wishing love.'
I concluded very softly. 'Now 'tis true. We are all one.'

CXXXIII.

"I spoke in solemn joy but not unmindful of a task
remaining to be settled. The queen must be confronted.
I summoned her and watched her turn as she responded
to my messenger. She took a great breath and everything
of her from ribs to eyebrows lifted and held in angry
readiness to strike. In surly indignation, surrounded
by an escort of her maids, she was brought across the hall.

CXXXIV.

"As the queen approached, I bid my love withdraw up a flight
to the landing to attend. 'Corverus, you have no right...'
Still twenty feet from me, the woman had begun her rant.
'I am your mother and the queen!' Seeing Lumine was safe
on the landing, I whirled to meet the woman eye to eye.
'I am Prince Plato now, and as such you will address me.
Be warned, woman, and give these words to Sinua, your lord.'

CXXXV.

"'My Lord!' she gasped. 'What are you saying?' She hung in mid-breath.
'Tell him that from this point on, he does nothing unobserved.
Faradonias, my steward, having re-established
the tree I have brought back, will train a horticulturist
to succeed himself, and then, with nine good men, all taking
my direct instruction, assume a warning surveillance,
constant observation of the doctor and his puppets.'

CXXXVI.

"'And such a puppet you would call me!' she blurted loudly.
'Silence and listen,' I said. 'Until Faradonias
can assume his new role, the doctor's under house arrest,
with a list of exercises and restrictions given
him before this day is done. The sooner he is docile
to my purposes, the sooner the guards replace their swords
in scabbards. Give him this message without embellishment.'

CXXXVII.

"'How dare you place the doctor under the authority
of that small unentertaining man. He's a commoner.'
'Only by birth,' I said. 'Were I not at last returned,
he would be my dying father's worthiest successor.
I am not ignorant of my kingdom, nor of your role.'
'And what that is, I will not deign to ask my son,' she snarled.
'I labored your birth to be murdered with ingratitude.'

CXXXVIII.

"'The body I've been given incubated in your womb,
and you yet have your place, to be my father's eyes and ears,
though ever yet obedient to his mind. Perception
of a certain range is your specialty; we can use it,
though what you make of your perceptions is untrustworthy,
self-centered, and too outlandish ever to be enthroned.
Go now. Call your seamstresses to dress you for the wedding.

CXXXIX.

"I turned from the queen and mounted the stairs to the landing
where Lumine awaited in silent goodwill, her slight smile
welcoming me. I kissed her forehead as I held the crown
of her head in my palm. 'My love, by now you understand
our place in this household and land, who's for us, who's against,
and in the fixing of our fair authority, your will
must be as well asserted as my own. Clarity rules.

CXL.

"'At the ball following our wedding, I would have you dance
one waltz with Dr. Sinua. His every step will test
your resolve not to be defrauded of your role. Tell him
with defining firmness this message: he has his place here,
as minister to the health of our subjects, nothing more,
for our sacred task extends beyond his understanding.
He will resent you and burn before your eye. Hold your gaze.'

CXLI.

"She spoke, 'I promise, my lord. He will know who rules this house.'
I continued. 'Faradonias and his guard of nine
must be instructed and given the tools of their new work.
For each, three implements I'll fashion, all of most ancient
proven use, though each man must be an expert of them all.
With these tools in the hands of my steward's men, in the house
and in the land order will be reckoned and our work secured.'

CXLII.

"There on the landing of the stair, we held each other's gaze.
'I am married now, my lord. Tomorrow's ceremony
shares our state with all the residents, but I need no proof
beyond this joining. My will is yours to direct.' And I,
'And your love shapes the meaning of my service to the truth.'
There on the landing of the stair, we took these vows next day
before the lifted eyes of all. The rest is happiness.'"

CXLIII.

His story now finished, Jules exhaled a great stream of breath,
and we all relaxed the posture of our wonder and sank,
though but slightly, into delight and knowledge of delight.
No one spoke, as each became aware of what the story
had attracted. There surrounding our configuration
were some two dozen sets of eyes and ears, in no order,
at varying distances, but clear in their attention.

CXLIV.

Sheepishly, they shuffled on or turned their childlike faces
back to their own worlds. Beyond them, down the dim corridor,
slept the great snoring mass. That some had wakened to the tale,
we took as an encouraging sign. We stretched in our chairs
and looked with genuine fondness at each other's faces.
At last Anamusa spoke, "Jules, if I am to be next,
let us pause a bit. I am between awe and contentment."

End, Book Two

Book Three : *The Mast*

I.

The welcome rest proved dangerous, almost the undoing
of the enterprise, as finding refreshment at that hour
was difficult and engendered a willing wandering
among our number. Some found themselves in long corridors
of darkened shops, while other sauntered on in loosened aim
to distant terminals. I sat alone almost an hour
fighting sleep, but each return restored my fragile vigil.

II.

First came Marco and Mathilde, having found no nourishment.
"All windows closed. This world sleeps and needs us not," said Marco,
not without the briefest sigh. "To verify the waste of time
is a sharp shock." "To be often stings," said Mathilde gently,
then in wonder added, "but William, where are the others?"
"Perhaps they have discovered something," Marco interposed.
"One hopes they have not lost themselves to find it," said Mathilde.

III.

Two minutes in silence had we sat when Ruby joined us,
unperturbed, bright, lighter in mood than we. "No food," said she,
"but half an hour of long slow stretching strides relieves the spine."
I concurred, opining that a knotted neck casts a pall
on listening and seeing, closing down the corridors
of sense, just as a knotted lower back strangles breath.
She looked at me as if confronted by a mystery.

IV.

Before I had time to try to resolve her puzzlement,
Jules and Carroll reappeared, side by side and stride for stride.
"Any luck with food?" asked Marco as they both found their chairs
and carefully sat down. "I'm sorry, Marco," Carroll said,
patting his ample tummy, "food was not my need just now."
"Nor mine," Jules seconded. "We were discussing getting home,"
Carroll owned, "until we woke to our further wandering."

V.

"The future steals us into thought and prattle," Jules allowed.
"And the returning never ends," affirmed Mathilde, smiling.
"But where is Ana?" Ruby asked. "Did anyone see her?"
"We did not," replied Jules, speaking for himself and Carroll.
"Nor we," added Marco, "though had we, we ourselves might not
have wandered quite so far. "Should one of us go search for her?"
said Ruby in mild alarm but received no quick response.

VI.

When Carroll finally spoke, our attention was prepared
for listening. "I think we can agree it is not wise
to search without knowledge. Random seeking soon wastes itself
and most often ends in exhaustion, having forfeited
more than was collected. Anamusa is a student
of the Way and"—he chortled—"of the way back." We all smiled.
"So by your reasoning, Carroll, we sit and wait for her?"

VII.

"You're persistent, Ruby," Carroll said in commendation.
He continued, "If my reasoning is true, yet it has
but temporary application. I would say we wait
till we can wait no longer. At some point our missing her
will overcome our judgment. If the heart grows desperate,
reason is a low fence." So we sat, present to ourselves
and the empty chair, reining in emotions not yet named.

VIII.

Some minutes passed in this discomfort. None of us desired
to begin a conversation not including Ana.
At last Mathilde produced a subject both innocuous
and profound enough to let us speak. "Which of the angels
tethers Ana now?" she wondered. "Certainly they guard us
when we drift, and call us back, first with subtle flower scents,
and then with sharper sounds and pricks." Inwardly we thanked her.

IX.

"Anamusa is Greek," said Jules, "and she has promised us
a Greek story. Perhaps a Greek immortal summons her
back even as I speak. "It has been some time since we've heard
a Greek story," offered Marco. "It's true," confirmed Mathilde.
"I haven't read a Greek text in many months, but I'm sure
that Ana brings nothing tired or nostalgic to our game."
"The Greek influence lingers. We carry it with us," said Jules.

X.

"I meant to ask about your Prince Plato, Jules," Carroll said.
"The choice of name set me wondering. Nothing in your tale
was Greek except that name, so great, so prominently placed.
What was your intention?" After a moment of silence,
Jules thoughtfully replied, "I'd like to say the choice of name
was intentional, even more to say it was inspired,
but the truth is there it was on my tongue and in your ears."

XI.

"You had not chosen it before?" asked Marco and Mathilde
in unison. "I had not, though in the time since telling,
I've had thoughts about the way the story went. Plato called
us to a task, an ideal state, and though we've gone beyond
his writings on the soul, the task he called us to remains."
"Does your prince call us back to Plato's blueprint?" Carroll asked.
"I doubt it," Jules said, "but we must not forget that project."

XII.

"True, since our tools are so much sharper now," noted Marco.
"His story mentioned that," Mathilde affirmed. "Recall, Marco,"—
"Behold!" Ruby blurted in delight. "Anamusa walks
our way, and quite intently too, as I'm reading her face."
We all turned, attending her approach. Up to us she strode
and spoke as if there hadn't been an interval. "So, Jules,
why'd your story not include the frame that we'd agreed on?"

XIII.

Despite our best work at restraint, we failed at holding in
our laughter. Ana marveled as she filled her empty chair,
"So what have I interrupted? Have I been wandering
so long that a new discussion walks upright already?"
"We were worried about you," Ruby said in simpler words
than the rest of us would probably have used. Ana claimed,
"I returned as soon as my story seemed firm in my mind."

XIV.

"Are you ready to begin?" asked Ruby. 'I thought I was
some minutes ago, and so I started back," Ana said.
"But then the question I just asked of Jules entered my mind,
and I wondered if our ground rules had changed. So have they, Jules?"
"No, Ana," Jules replied. "Telling the tale in character
left me no way back to complete a frame. I feel lucky
just to have finished that unpremeditated closing."

XV.

"'Unpremediated art' is Milton's phrase," said Carroll.
"Yes," said Jules, "but Milton sat in the Poet's Chair. He spoke
inspired verse, the instrument of higher mind. I'm sitting
in a plastic airport chair, waiting out a storm, trying
not to fall asleep." "As are we all, friend," promised Carroll
in an encouraging tone. "All in all," Jules concluded,
'I'm glad the tale found a cogent end and let me speak it."

XVI.

"I think," offered Ana, "you underestimate your gift.
I was stunned by your story, as I told you, and at a loss
to follow you. And as I'd planned a tale of Odysseus,
who bore the title 'never at a loss', I quaked inside
and worried that I should abandon my far simpler work.
But finally I came to think that my tale is my tale,
as my life is my life, as we are friends and not rivals."

XVII.

"So we're ready to begin," reiterated Ruby.
"Be patient, dear," said Ana soothingly, then going on,
"so at that point I turned and headed here, but the question
still sounded intermittently, and as you heard, burst forth
all too bluntly as soon as Jules' face came into view.
Like my soul, my narration needs our rules. My aim's to please
and hold and nothing in my tale originates with me."

XVIII.

Touched by Ana's words, we understood her absence and felt
a sympathetic gladness that she was back among us.
There's little better for the heart than loss of vanity.
Heaven is in control, and defeated expectation
and the wonder at what befalls us, are the first steps back
to being Heaven's audience attending our own lives.
Those lives go on as Heaven wills: our watching is our prayer.

XIX.

Ana then continued, "Mathilde and Jules have put in place
the pillars of the temple; to their companion pieces
we will add our ornaments, the first of which, my story,
will present Odysseus wrestling with the greatest foe
bedeviling man, the siren call that satisfies us
even as it locks the throat in airless talking, freezes
the eyeballs in their sockets, stops the ears and dooms the soul."

XX.

"We all know what that is," said Marco. "It is a grim shock
to hear it so chillingly described." "There is an impulse
in my lower spine," said Carroll, "to stand and move away,
disengage from you and let a lighter curiosity
lead me down the hall." "And in three steps," Marco added,
"you know where you would be—right back in your 'airless talking'."
'Precisely," Carroll concurred. "Ana has scared the devil."

XXI.

"Anamusa," Ruby uttered sheepishly, "Could you wait
to start your story until I'm sure that what's just been said
is clear to me. My usual impatience has been quashed."
We gladly gave her our attention, and she continued,
"I think I understand that you mean what our teaching calls
imagination, ungoverned daydreaming, do you not?
I don't know it as the strangling disease that you've described."

XXII.

"Time and self-observation will avail you," Carroll said.
"But you might as well be talking about fatal cancer.
The condition you pictured is death, not daydreaming."
Ruby's voice quavered. "If you're saying that my inner talk
and wandering mind are deadly, then I am surely lost."
Patiently Ana gathered herself to answer. "Be calm.
All that's changed is your view of the problem's enormity."

XXIII.

"Then what has been my error?" Ruby asked with a poignance
we could not ignore. The audible desperation
in her voice and her palpable effort to control it
would have elicited compassion from the hardest heart.
There was a moment of silence in which all the older ones—
Ana, Carroll, Marco, Mathilde and Jules—exchanged glances.
"How long have you been with us, Ruby?" Carroll gently asked.

XXIV.

"For nine months now," Ruby answered, "but it feels much longer."
Her answer shocked me as I realized that even I,
the baby of this blessed company, had almost been
as long as she in the teaching. Was I just as naïve
to the real danger of the vagrant mind? Without the calm
the older ones maintained, Ruby's sincere perplexity
could have been contagious. I steadied myself for trial.

XXV.

"First, be assured," Carroll began, " that your understanding
is not wrong but merely childlike, as you are but a child
in this work, a toddler who can walk on uncertain feet
a few precarious paces. What then happens? You stop
and lean upon a wall where fascination fixes you
until an accidental waking spurs a few more steps."
Ruby confessed, "Truly your words describe my poverty."

XXVI.

"Not poverty but youth. Beware of self-judgment wriggling
like a worm into word choice and inflection," noted Jules.
"However long it takes to reach maturity, be firm
in knowing you've begun a sacred labor." Ruby smiled
with the effort of gratitude, but all could sense her fear.
"I know this is holy ground," she said softly, looking up,
"but the footing is so doubtful, just as Carroll tells us."

XXVII.

As they spoke, I felt the words come bubbling up from within
and without quick restraint might have interrupted Ruby;
then into the first available space jumped my question.
"Tell me please, how is a wandering mind so dangerous?"
"Ah," Carroll mused, "our young souls are at once scared of the truth
and eager for it. This situation is very right
for teaching. May we older ones be worthy of the call."

XXVIII.

"Let us expose the topic carefully and thoroughly.
We are not in a hurry, and here more than anywhere
haste is a gift from the devil," said Mathilde firmly.
Marco replied admiringly, "You speak with strength, my love."
"As must we all to hold our course," affirmed Mathilde. "Well gripped
oars are necessary here. The wind's too shifty for sail."
Marco gazed at his spouse with deep respect, as did we all.

XXIX.

"Please go on, Mathilde," said Jules. "You speak with authority."
She took two intentional breaths. "I will sound the first note;
then others can prolong the effort till the truth is out.
When the mind begins to wander, already we are lost.
Already has the lower self dislodged the soul whose home
is presence, only presence: the guardian has been duped;
the impersonator has come to sit upon the throne."

XXX.

She paused, and Ruby spoke up politely, "Something in me
feels the truth in your words, but the metaphors confound me.
Could you be more clinical, like the books we begin with?"
"I'm sorry," Mathilde smiled. "As our studies over the years
 have grown more focused on the keys to sacred texts, I find
their poetry becomes my speech. Let me say it this way:
the lower self seeks with every breath to distract the mind."

XXXI.

"Then I am right to be afraid," said Ruby. Jules replied,
"The fear is just another tool by which it takes control.
If fear is in you, be aware of it and stand your ground."
He added gently, "Fear is an excess of energy."
"So I sit paralyzed in fear of a wandering mind.
It is too ironical," said Ruby. "What a thick knot
am I tied by, hanging here strangling. Surely I must die."

XXXII.

"In your own understanding is the grip of salvation,"
charged Anamusa, her voice dominant on certain breath.
"You see your condition. What you see, you don't have to be."
The whole configuration fell mirthful at her slogan,
but Ana pressed on fervently. "The knot is actual.
It constricts your breath, clenches your throat, and stops eyes and ears
from scanning the world. Can you not feel it tightening?"

XXXIII.

"In our enthusiasm to explain, we trip," said Jules.
Carroll cleared his throat as if to call the world's attention.
"Let us examine soberly what a wandering mind
truly is. What happens to produce imagination?
We have all been taught that uncontrolled mind activity,
that which we call imagination, is a chief weapon
in the arsenal of the body's master brain." He paused.

XXXIV.

"More metaphors," said Ruby "My old life was a battle,
and my new one's taught in holy poems about battles.
Does the fighting ever end? I am very tired of it."
"My sympathy for you is palpable," consoled Carroll.
"Perhaps I can explain without the imagery of strife,
though you must never think our lives on this path can be based
but in struggle and effort. If not war, yet always work."

XXXV.

"Go on," said Ruby. "You will have my best attention."
Carroll began in earnest. "The functions of the body
are controlled by the instinctive brain. Of the realm of flesh
it is the rightful ruler and must gauge in each moment
how much of its alertness is required. It does its job
unconfused by morality or love, though it can cloak
itself in either. Its interest is its own survival."
'This I have been taught," said Ruby, but why use the pronoun 'it'?"

XXXVI.

"I speak of animal nature," Carroll continued,
the earthly part of man, itself on earth its sole concern.
This brain—which we mythologize as Satan—determines
breath to breath which functions are needed and what energy
should be available to them." "We do have things to do
in the world," Ruby affirmed. "True," he went on, "but rarely
do we call upon the body's fully focused labor."

XXXVII.

"So," said Ruby, "when it is not needed, the mind can play.
That begins to make sense. But what is the mechanism?"
'What do you mean?" Ana asked. "There must be a switch to throw
or a valve to close," Ruby declared. "It's all mechanics."
"You are correct," said Carroll, "but to us it seems seamless
and immediate. We rarely can observe the mind shift
from purposeful focus to self-indulgent wandering."

XXXVIII.

"We come to ourselves later in the wastes of time," said Jules.
'That I have experienced," said Ruby. "It's unnerving."
"Here's what we know: consciousness must always be asserted;
stop and the drift begins, and we awake somewhere down river."
Carroll's declaration ushered in attentive silence.
After a moment, he resumed. "When the assertion comes
from the heart, it is prayer; from above, it is God's judgment."

XXXIX.

"Prayer I understand," said Ruby, "and I've been instructed
in the art, which is much different from what I practiced
in my former life, but the phrase 'God's judgment' troubles me.
It provokes the fear of punishment I had as a child."
"Yes," said Jules, "so much of our knowledge is cloaked in language
the world reads literally and thereby lives in darkness.
To be perturbed with metaphors is part of your salvation."

XL.

"'God's judgment'," Carroll offered, " is consciousness extended,
prolonged over moments or minutes by its refusal
to be other than itself. Through its steward it rejects
all the body's blandishments, which come as fluttering thoughts
and curious questions and urgent promptings from below.
What the world's great religions call the Last Day or Judgment
is the God in you being God, repudiating time."

XLI.

With the care one takes in walking when holding close a babe,
Ruby chose her words. "The state you describe—God being God—
I have only known as a fleeting visitor, a gift,
which never comes without wonder rising to tug at it."
Jules spoke gravely. "The thing we've called Satan or the devil
will assail even that state, dragging down its perfect love,
soiling it with vanity. You see, Satan would be God."

XLII.

"The sacred cosmic drama is played out within each.
Each of us a universe," said Marco, "conscious or dead."
"So when the mind wanders," Ruby affirmed, "it traverses
a dead landscape, reshuffling the past to make the future.
"Yes," Jules intoned, "imaginary living satisfies us."
"That is clear, " said Ruby, "but what did Anamusa mean
to speak of hangman's knots, clenched throats, eyes and ears obstructed?"

XLIII.

"Ruby, you may get your mechanism yet," Carroll smiled.
Anamusa turned to align herself with Ruby's eyes.
"I will try to be simple. The mind can only wander
when the senses are occluded. Imagination begins
with the same imperceptible tightening of the throat
as if to speak, and soon we are speaking—internally—
and the ears and the eyes stop up to listen and make pictures."

XLIV.

"My God!" Ruby exclaimed. "You mean we're talking to ourselves,
looking at and listening to illustrated stories."
"Whenever the body's master brain determines it safe
to rest from attention," Ana went on, "the throat tightens,
the vocal apparatus engages within, a tale
commences, and off we go, pleasing ourselves aimlessly
or troubling ourselves needlessly till attention returns."

XLV.

"And the shift," said Marco, "is automatic, too subtle
for the will, too immediate for the observing mind."
"Before we know it," added Jules, "we've slipped into the noose."
"Perhaps too many metaphors," Mathilde admonished all,
but Ruby spoke up firmly, "And you may call it a noose
because it grips the neck, the throat, closing down the senses—
strangling out the present, sending us wandering from God."

XLVI.

"That's it, Ruby!" said the older ones in happy chorus.
But here I had to intervene. "One thing remains unclear.
Are we attentive only when the master brain permits?"
Carroll quickly collected himself. "We must distinguish
conscious attention from mere mechanical alertness.
Being present to oneself, aware of one's attention,
is a conscious effort ever requiring renewal."

XLVII.

"I understand the constant labor of remembering,
but are all our efforts hostage to the body?" I asked.
"The soul knows itself by separation," Marco offered,
"by becoming aware of itself as not the body.
So yes, the body is necessary; its attention—
what Carroll more rightly called alertness—is the rude ground
from which the toiling soul ascends by our ancient practice."

XLVIII.

"We are instructed men," said Jules, "and the result is life
as an internal striving after consciousness, the growth
of the soul. The body's master brain is our resistance,
an intelligence not to be dismissed, which by its nature
begrudges and obstructs the tax of any energy
that fuels our higher project. We have our instruction;
the body has its own indulgent ways: such is the work."

XLIX.

"The body is a grave in which men are content to live,
satisfied by the false freedom of a wandering mind,
the misuse of hope, and the unconscious ease of belief.
But you children need no more testimony," said Mathilde.
"By the grace of Heaven, we know what we know, and only
Heaven itself knows why we've been trusted with the knowledge;
but having learned what we know, we cannot live otherwise."

L.

Carroll looked straight across at Anamusa. "The prelude
to your story seems to be sounding its last sweetened notes."
"Yes," she answered, "my tale is at the brink of readiness,
and I hope you will all enjoy it. An offhand comment
by the Teacher in the early years caused me to conceive
the idea, which gestated slowly as our studies
connected our work to a tradition of consciousness."

LI.

Marco continued the thread. "Part of a true teacher's task
is to reveal the teaching as a manifestation
of an ongoing presence in the world. From early on,
we were given the names of conscious beings who attend us:
recent ones like Andersen and Lewis Carroll, to whom
we've paid tribute tonight, and earlier ones going back
through history to Joseph, who brought Abraham's seed to Egypt."

LII.

"Among the figures who make sense of history for us
is Homer," Ana added. The epics under his name
bear the signs of conscious authorship; an awakened soul
produced them, and as I am Greek, I have always held them
in high regard. So my story is derived from Homer,
an expansion on an episode crucial to the progress
of Odysseus, whose adventures dramatize self-knowledge."

LIII.

"And if Ana's story pleases and instructs," said Marco
taking turn, "then we'll be ready for mine, which will follow
hers immediately, with no further introduction."
"So the effort to frame the tales, which I did not complete,
is now to be abandoned altogether?" queried Jules.
"Actually not," said Ana. "I will begin a frame
which Marco promises to finish when his tale is done."

LIV.

"Most intriguing," Carroll mused. "So your tales are twins that fit
in a single frame. Is your also Homeric, Marco?"
"Not exactly," Marco said. Mine's from the New Testament."
"I wonder if Homer ever imagined a pairing
with an Evangelist," said Jules mirthfully. "I presume
Marco's story will focus on Jesus rather than Paul."
"First Odysseus," said Ana. "Hold yourselves steady and hear."

LV.

"As scholarship must be affirming," she began, "not proud
or parasitic, I studied what later ages made
of Homer's stories. Did other minds find in him the God
we recognize, and drink his tales as nectar for the soul?"
In fact I found in late antiquity among the group
Augustine was so nurtured by, the Neoplatonists,
an understanding of the soul's progress in Homer's works.

LVI.

"Perhaps I should say 'work', for *The Odyssey* is greater
in this vein than *The Iliad*; written second, it holds
a complete map of self-mastery in the allegory
of the Ithacan's adventures. And I was delighted
to discover the tradition of reading Homer thus
extends through time to William Blake, another finished man
we honor, whose *Sea of Time and Space* instructs my practice.

LVII.

"My own thoughts on this method began when I was still new
among us and read the Teacher's thought that the Siren's song
could be imagination, in those days not thought to be
so great an obstacle as now we know. Next came Cyclops:
that is, remembering from school that his name meant 'wheel eye',
I realized that being trapped in Cyclops' cave described
the soul's imprisonment from which Odysseus finds escape."

LVIII.

"Ana, please slow down," requested Ruby. "I know the plot
of the Cyclops story, but the connections you have found
come too fast for me." Mathilde concurred, "I am also lost."
'Excuse me, Ana said. "I should be more deliberate.
Let me begin again. The cave is a common symbol
of the earth which even Plato uses. To be trapped there
is to be earthbound, time bound, mortal in body and mind."

LIX.

"Yes, that makes sense. Please go on," said Mathilde. "I add to that
the image of the wheel—the cycle in the Cyclops' eye—
and the giant himself, whom Homer draws uncivilized.
Confined thus, Odysseus escapes the fate of all mankind."
"What is that?" asked Ruby. Ana concluded, "To live
by instinct, trapped on earth in the cycle of birth and death."
"I presume, " said Jules, "you find much meaning in the method."

LX.

Ana smiled. "He crafts a weapon to wound the brute monster
in the forehead, even as David wounded Goliath,
and hidden by a flock of sheep, he and his men depart."
"After the giant himself has rolled away the stone," said Jules.
"Free from the cave but far from home," Carroll reminded us.
"I cite this episode as a way of reading Homer.
It may help," said Ana, "with what you are about to hear."

LXI.

"I am aware my all-too-fast-unfolding tale confounds
a few, and you listen with unequal understanding.
Still I believe that if launched well, this narrative will bring
its hearers to unity, like the rowers in a boat
who begin awkwardly with uneven rhythm but soon
are synchronized in perfect effort. Thus to Odysseus
returning from Hades to seek Circe's counsel once more.

LXII.

"Only the greatest heroes return from the death journey:
Herakles, and lucky Theseus, Orpheus without his bride;
later Virgil's pious man of arms and pilgrim Dante.
One cannot challenge the dominion of the secret king
without becoming changed, sobered, unimpressed with the world.
Thus our man beached at Aiaia, beyond fatigue, at dusk
on the longest day of his life and waited for the dawn.

LXIII.

"The morning was no shock to him, as duty to his friend
had kept him ready. Elpenor's body, claimed and buried
beneath his upright oar, had respect, and then the enchantress
could come down with provisions, taking our man aside
to warn him of the next dangers—the Sirens, whose singing
lured sailors to wreck on wasting rocks where they died dangling
from spars of their own vessels, still smitten with what they'd heard.

LXIV.

"And if Odysseus lived and sailed on, a choice would follow,
which Circe would not advise upon, only promising
that either way would bring more trials. As a man returned
from death he listened, his fear by memory's rule annulled.
Her instructions were crisp and clear, and the welcomed knowledge
buoyed him and he obeyed as he heard. Her final warning—
not to touch the Cattle of the Sun—brought strange bitterness.

LXV.

"With eagerness harnessed to clarity, he took to ship,
storing close on deck a wheel of beeswax and rolls of line.
Circe's benevolent magic provided perfect winds
for the journey, so quickly under a controlled sail,
he convened the men on the steady deck for a warning.
He told them of the Sirens and the song they must not hear,
and with truth made the coming dangers intimate to them.

LXVI.

They did not shiver to shake off his words but received them
soberly in readiness, and the instant that he stopped,
the wind stopped also, and the men moved to their oars, needing
no new orders. With deliberate speed, Odysseus warmed
nuggets of wax in his supple hands, and the rising sun
assisted him; then he walked down the line of his oarsmen,
bracing them, filling their ears with the blessing of silence.

LXVII.

"Then he signaled six of his best and gave them the strong rope.
At the mast they gathered, where two of them stood resolute
while he climbed to their shoulders and steadied his back and neck
against the great pole. Two others in symmetry stood firm
while Eurylokos ascended with rope to their shoulders
and lashed his captain down, doublingly circling his broad chest,
looping under his staunch trunk and over his bent-back arms.

LXVIII.

"Having secured the master to the mast, Eurylokos,
not without a secret thrill at seeing great Odysseus
so constrained, handed the line ends down to Perimedes
who stretched them taught behind and fastened them five full paces
back to stern. Their work complete, these six most trusted shipmates
made their way back to their oars and resumed their rhythmic work.
His spine flattened to the mast, patient Odysseus waited.

LXIX.

"He scanned the calm horizon as the half-risen sun lit
every color the shining sea could make, its crystal flecks
darting up and out from the waving sheet of lapis blue.
The rough ropes chafed his inner thighs and shoulders, but he used
the irritation, directed it in mind to incite
his senses, prompt their best acuity, so that relaxed
in vigilance, he attended what Heaven would reveal.

LXX.

"And there! port side far, far ahead, a cloud touched the sea line.
Soon the men could see it and understood their task, to pass
it open-eyed but deaf and without breathing its vapor.
Perimedes gauged the distance and set a careful course.
The master felt more keenly the rigid pole that straightened
his spine, and he held his head erect and extended deep
the current of his breathing. He ordered himself, 'Hold course'.

LXXI.

"The ship slid on, by the attraction of the mystery
urged to port but by will of master and instructed crew
bending barely to starboard. In this tension they approached
the floating cloud. 'But where is the song?' wondered Odysseus.
'Where is the danger of which Circe warned? A nuzzling fog
is no temptation to a man who's taken the beatings
I've had from the Gods. I know my strength, and here is no threat.'

LXXII.

"'*You are right, bold Odysseus. Your force of will is too great
for our poor allurements.*' The words came in a whispered voice,
tender and musical, from out of the fog to his ear.
His head turned left to let his eyes seek a source of the voice,
but nothing visible shone through the comforting cloud.
'*You are the man of weapons and might. You have our envy,
and so we are yours to command. You may ask all we know.*'

LXXIII.

"Squinting left into the fog, the bound master felt his neck
stiffen and his eyes glaze and grow rigid in their sockets.
'Turn from this deception,' he told himself, and forced his gaze
back to the distant strait directly on. His neck relaxed,
and a deeper breath moved easily past his throat.
The ship kept moving past the island, though there was no isle
to be seen. All on the left was impenetrable mist.

LXXIV.

"*'Monsters await you there ahead, dear friend. No choice for man,
Scylla or Charibdis.'* The whisper returned to his ear,
but now with a note of sorrow and piteous lament.
*'What choice is it to be a bloody meal or a drowned corpse?
Do not look. Do not think about which men will die screaming
in the narrow passage. Destruction soon enough will be
present upon you, bearing down. Straight ahead is horror.'*

LXXV.

"The master looked down from his height at his dutiful crew,
obedient in their labor, rowing in synchrony.
*'Do not ask which ones you will consign to grisly doom.
If you would know the future, then ask us of its blessing:
of your return to Ithaca in glory, the embrace
of your faithful wife, the manliness of your son now grown.
While there's time, let us sing of your favor among the gods.'*

LXXVI.

"'All vanity,' he said aloud, though no man could hear him.
'Would I trade my soul for vanity? Better these rope cuts
on my shoulders and thighs. They are small sufferings but real.
Your praises and promises are grand deceits, death to men
who sail. The mast straightening my back bends not to vain lies.'
*'You are beyond brave, Odysseus. We see now why your wife
so long endures, bold before the graspers threatening her.'*

LXXVII.

"Penelope appeared in pain before the Master's eyes
with a look of brave beseeching that stabbed his heart and bid
him cry out to her, but he caught himself and turned his face
right to the horizon. 'Leave this mirage of a woman.
She is all my hope, but I must hold tighter to the truth
of not knowing. I am here, and she is not.' The rowers
kept unbroken rhythm with their strokes, and the ship sailed on.

LXXVIII.

"As if reprieved from hanging, the noose removed, breath returned
to him, Odysseus thanked Heaven with a quick skyward glance
and felt again the chafing ropes and the knots in his back.
'You're not my father,' said a voice behind. No whisper this,
a real voice, though puerile, unwilling to be masculine.
*'I have no father in this world. I will not be the son
of a vagrant coward whose home is famously debauched.'*

LXXIX.

"The master's breath went slack. He gave his ears to the longing
to hear more, and the strident contemptuous voice resumed.
*'You have no face, abandoner, but I wish you could be
in this ruined hall to see these men, food in their beards
and wine stains on their tunics, take their rutting turns with her
who was your wife, while some of the lesser ones fondle me.
Your house is a landmark in Greece, fatherland of heroes.'*

LXXX.

"Odysseus bristled and strained to turn to the voice, to confront
the foul inciter, but the ropes held and burned, and he knew
to waste his strength no further. The thought of Telemachus
angry and unlearned in manhood humbled him, emptied him
of heart, made baubles of his victories. 'If this is true,
and my name is less than nothing, my wife and son defiled,
still I look on here, whatever I am beneath a name.'

LXXXI.

"'*You are nothing but a lie, Odysseus, only worthy*
to be laughed at. You have killed your child.' The voice departed
before the master could frame another thought, and his heart
was a wound inside him. 'I would kneel to you, O Heaven,
but even the solace of submission is denied me.'
'*The greatest of heroes still have need of consolation.*'
This voice, soothing and feminine, came as if from within.

LXXXII.

"'*You have passed the test, Odysseus. Look left. The fog abates.*
The muscles of your loyal crew have brought you through the mist
and still they stoutly labor. Give the signal of release.
Come down from your watchtower. Your swollen rope burns need salve,
your joints need gentle handling, and you need rest from the weight
you have carried so long. In the well earned sleep of heroes,
we'll come to you, who regards not his own great suffering.'

LXXXIII.

"The tired master's head dipped to his chest, and in his heart
came sweet relenting, and the signal would have been given
had not interposed in his mind the memory of storm
and roaring when Aeolus' bag of winds had been opened.
He had been asleep only to be knocked awake and tossed
about the deck by the tempest loosed by his gullible crew.
Up surging came the great man's spirit: he lifted his eyes.

LXXXIV.

"'Not to comfort will I give my being,' he spoke aloud.
'True to my instruction I remain. You may not have me,
honeyed voices, and your phantom hands will not make mere flesh
of me. I am tired, and tired men are weak, and your talons
were fashioned by the Gods to seize the weakened hearts of men.
I sail on past tempting and the cravings you give hope to.'
The mist had dissolved, and the still climbing sun owned the sky.

LXXXV.

"And there came a quiet moment, a respite, a silence
around the master in which he knew himself in Heaven,
in common with its Godly residents, a peace prolonged
that made the sky beauteous in itself, and the blue sea
a wonder to the eye: not Odysseus now, no longer
he the mortal bound in mortal suffering to the mast,
but an uplifted gaze complete in single sense, and still.

LXXXVI.

"But soon wriggling between unlabored breaths came a small thought:
'How great a trial is over now!' And to this thought
a chorus came, as parched throats to water, and continued,
'Think now of homecoming and Penelope's soft embrace.'
'Or a fire in your great hall on which roasts succulent cuts
while your manly son listens in awe to your heroes' tales.'
'Odysseus, you have triumphed. Look back on all you've conquered.'

LXXXVII.

"Grave suspicion rose in the man, and once again he felt
the burning ropes. 'Restrain vagrant mind,' he cautioned himself.
'Do not take lightly Circe's warnings and waste her guidance.
More horrors await. Be vigilant.' He noted the crew
whose unabated strokes swept back the water; their breathing
labored, and their aching torsos faint grunts and sighs expelled,
but there was no stopping, no slackening their rhythmic art.

LXXXVIII.

"*'Well done, Odysseus, a rare redemption,'* said a voice
of friendly femininity. *'Our isle is far behind*
and still you stand alert, permitting no homecoming thoughts,
no self-congratulation. But neither dare you wonder
what you've lost, what you could have tasted bare minutes ago
but now is gone forever. All knowledge past and future
with us lies in our tender care to share with those we love.'

LXXXIX.

"The muscles of the master bristled and the taste of loss
rose in his throat. 'Back to your fog; no more deceiving now.'
The words struggled, but that slumping weight of never knowing
all he'd longed to know came over him like leaden shadow.
With wearying surprise, he forced the helpless question out,
'What right have you to tempt me here and now? I made the choice
to repel you and leave your lying cloud of promises.'

XC.

"*'Yes, Odysseus, you made the choice then, to leave the knowledge
that we offered you behind, but we remain with you now
and ever, to the end of your manhood, reminding you
of what you have forsaken. What a childish heart you have
to believe your task so simple. Tie yourself to the mast,
sail past a foggy patch of sea, then be forever free!
The envelope of flesh is strong, the Sirens stronger still.'*

XCI.

"The sobered hero held himself. What his eyes were seeing
he acknowledged, and the sounds in his ears he knew as sounds.
*'Very good, Odysseus! Defend yourself. Keep your senses
monitored and clean. But my sweet voice is deeper in you
than the lines of sense. You refused us, would not dwell with us,
so we have taken residence in you. Deep in your throat,
inaccessible to surgery, we hold our sessions.'*

XCII.

"'I'm not unmindful. You cannot make me think about you.'
He spoke softly but aloud. 'Though you have infected me,
you have not conquered me, nor can you make me spread your plague.
And when my flesh gives up its grip, you'll remain trapped within.'
*'Fine speech, noble Odysseus! But how can you speak to us
and not have us in mind? Tie two telling words together,
nay, two syllables, and you've saddled horses for our ride.'*

XCIII.

"Another voice more like his own dear mother's claimed his ear.
*'We love you, Odysseus, and we give you food against loss
and comfort in your pain. Drop your eyes in discouragement,
let your chin sink to your breast, and we are there. Our faithful
singing dresses life in meaning when your prayers bring nothing.'*
'You demon liars! The thing you feed is not Odysseus
but an image, all vanity. I renounce that creature.'

XCIV.

"*'And where's the real Odysseus? Is it he who now protests
our hospitality, or he who loves Penelope,
or he who dared to maim that wheel-eyed brute, or he who joined
fair Circe in a whole year of purple-sheeted pleasure?'*
'I think the true Odysseus contrived the Trojan horse,'
said another voice, even more admiring. *'Nestled there
within the walls, he did to Troy what we do now to him.'*

XCV.

"*'Ah, a wonderful analogy!'* the motherly voice
in praise proclaimed. And thus the voices had their party,
a festival of table chat, to which their Odysseus
played befuddled auditor. Had not a clap of thunder
shaken the clear sky and a sudden bolt of lightening pierced
the horizon, the master might have spent a kidnapped hour.
Shocked awake, he saw the high-walled strait far off but coming.

XCVI.

"'Hanged and humiliated is he who'd be a hero.
Then let them have Odysseus, his proud thoughts, his vanity;
let the carrion eaters feast on the lie of his name.
Here am I, great Gods, nothing but your slave cleaned of craving.
I call to you without hope, I address you, I praise you,
for thus am I made, and if my call is pure, unceasing,
you who have made me cannot but hear me, such as I am.'

XCVII.

"Another lightening bolt from nowhere in the cloudless sky
flashed in the blue, bright as the sun, as if a messenger.
Through his eyes it seared straight to his brain, illuminating
all his mind as if it were a seamless whitened fabric.
And thereupon he watched in instantaneous display
the trials to come, the coming into being of destined things,
high sorrowful, had that which watched been made with fleshy heart.

XCVIII.

"He saw the gullet of the maelstrom, cauldron Charibdis,
spuming then swallowing, devouring all that floated near,
sucking acres of salt sea into its downward spiral.
He saw the oars of his frightened crew crossing, clattering
in chaos against the ship, as cold fear slackened their strength.
He saw their bold recovery, their unity of will
that turned the ship and drove it past the whirlpool's fatal reach.

XCIX.

"He saw them all cheering, exulting in brief victory,
as unaware they moved in range of Scylla's bloody strike.
Her twelve tentacles held up six heads, whose flesh-hungry mouths
were merciless in their grip, claiming the six best crewmen
from each passing ship, snatching and chewing and dripping gore.
He saw the dangling feet of his dear friends, caught and murdered
in mid-breath, recede up the cliff wall to her gaping door.

C.

"He saw the landing of a battered ship full of sick men
on sunny Thrinakia, isle holy to Helios.
He saw their grim council when their stores had dwindled and wind
would not come and food was all they wanted, how they gathered
round Eurylokos and listened to his forbidden plan.
He saw them roasting the meat of the God's sacred cattle,
barely able to wait to finish fatal sacrilege.

CI.

"All this the master beheld, absorbed in a brain's instant
faster than measure, and still more dire events were revealed.
He saw the storm of the vengeful Sun God and the struggle
of his drowning crew, washing down their last unholy meal
with gulps of salt water, and the mast of his splintered ship
floating past and beckoning him bestride it, taking him
back toward Charibdis, Circe's warnings recklessly wasted.

CII.

"He saw the fig tree, its saving branch extended, his hands
around it in life-giving grip, the mast re-emerging
from the whirlpool, the endless horizon of open sea,
at last the nine-days-distant isle, and then no more was seen.
With a start he returned to his flesh, the burns of the ropes,
and the men standing and stretching, removing the wax
from their ears, looking to him—the master—for direction.

CIII.

"Perimedes came to him, untied him, and helped him down
from his painful elevation. He gently rubbed the neck
and shoulders of his lord, holding each arm at the elbow
to stretch the muscles so long cramped in unrelenting toil.
Odysseus gazed at his shipmate with the agonized love
a father has for a young son he is sending to war,
knowing the boy too heartstrong and brave to return alive.

CIV.

"With an overbrimming heart, the master spoke to his friend:
'Perimedes, death is but a part of fate. We are here
facing death but ignorant of what the soul will greet next
in its long journey home. You are a worthy man who keeps
his fear from rising to his mind. For you death is a step
onto a bridge, a bold surefooted stride with no look back.'
The younger man listened in undiscerning gratitude.

CV.

"Then without restraint upon them surged cocksure Eurylokos,
demanding rudely of the master what was next to do.
'Odysseus, you've had your private session with the Sirens,
which none of the rest of us was worthy of. Satisfied
now you must be and ready to tell us whereto from here.
We've done your bidding faithfully; now where is our reward?
My appetite rises and overwhelms obedience.'

CVI.

"Odysseus flared inwardly but absorbing patiently
the heat of anger, he met Eurylokos eye to eye.
'This appetite of yours will eat your soul. Get hold of it
before you find yourself brazenly addressing Heaven
as you now address me. I'm but a man. Your impudence
wants more than I can give you, so the Gods must answer you.'
Dumbfounded, Eurylokos withdrew, eyes down, muttering.

CVII.

"Summoning the crew's attention, Odysseus spoke,
and his words were pure and terrible with a truth past all
human sentiment. The men listened with due gravity
and duty, and what they heard quickened highest sense, charged them
to true identity; no longer crew, no longer Greeks,
nor men, nor flesh, nor feeling, each knew himself at last,
an attending awareness awkward in a fated form.

CVIII.

"'There in clear sight stands the strait to which we steer, unknowing
which six will give their lives for the rest. The horror we will know
is human, confronting that which is pitiless to men.
The impossible decisions reveal that all is fate,
a stronger power's doing. We hope for meaning but see
past hope. Bodies die, in prime or age, but the ready part
which hears my words and knows their truth cannot die. So onward.'

CIX.

"Alert and open-eyed, shoulder to shoulder, thirty minds
as one in readiness they stood as the ship, her sails tied,
moved on the waves' current the last brief distance to the strait.
And then they were in through the narrow portal, offering
themselves to the high cliff walls and Heaven's stern commandments.
Straight above in its high noon, the sun illuminated
the ancient steeps and ledges of the craggy escarpments.

CX.

"And here and there, left and right, up the faces of the cliffs
were caves from which the winds seemed to whistle and moan, and birds
in undulating flocks would whirl in and out, their shrill cries
infrequent, withheld, barely heard above the constant beat
of air beneath their countless wings. Odysseus, gazing up,
maintained a steady, silent breathing and a focused eye,
preparing for the terror that he knew he must endure.

CXI.

"The ship had almost stopped in the water, inching forward
imperceptibly. Knowing that their progress must not halt,
the master, making silent gestures from his flowing hands,
designated six good men to take close seats behind oars
and row softly with slow extended strokes. As they obeyed,
Odysseus understood himself the agent of their fate,
for these six, unresisting, would soon give up their lives.

CXII.

"The slim passage narrowed further till the oars almost touched
the rocks on either side, but then the walls seemed to relax,
spread, and the ship entered a pool of sun-warmed clarity,
which seemed itself a kind of goal. How tempting to rest here,
to anchor, bathe, anoint one's hair and head and feet with oil
and give the afternoon to healing sleep. Here above all
the men needed a master, and he signaled them onward.

CXIII.

"A few rhythmic oarstrokes on, the sound began, a murmur,
a gutteral rumbling, as if the throat of earth were paused
on the brink of swallowing. The ship made an unwilled turn
to starboard and gathered speed till there beneath the cliff wall
stretched the insatiable hole of Charibdis sucking in
its next meal. Close enough they came to this shortcut to hell
to smell the sulfur burning and hear the echoing groans.

CXIV.

"Quick to their oarseats scrambled all the crew behind the six
already there. In full muscled toil, holding nothing back,
they pulled as their master against his own heart steered them left
toward Scylla yet unseen. 'The ship dies surprised and swallowed
all at once or sees her men devoured six by six,' he thought.
'Where are the Gods? The straight path is an aim impossible.'
And he watched as every hand gripped its tool in taut struggle.

CXV.

"From behind came a quaking wave and rain of foul debris
as the whirlpool vomited back its meal, thrusting the ship
across to the opposing cliff wall. Shuddering, heaving,
the noble craft came to rest as the surge spent itself out.
In measured caution, the bruised men unclenched their fisted hands,
straightened their wrenched necks and looked about to find their master,
who surprised them with his sword already drawn and lifted.

CXVI.

"The master watched himself; his body's movements were to him
as an observed performance: the hilt of his sword in hand,
the right arm upraised, the ready brain in watchful waiting.
'Odysseus,' Perimedes called, 'what are you poised to fight?'
The master guided his eyes left to right across the deck,
across the strait to the still foaming gorge of Charibdis,
and then ascending slightly, his gaze found a tiny ledge.

CXVII.

"And on the ledge stood dwarfed and stooped in age a battered tree—
could it be the fig tree of his vision?—and from its trunk
a branch extended, a vantage into the mouth of hell.
His right hand tightened its grip on the sword hilt, and the left
formed a clutching fist, as if to greet the branch they'd cling to.
Carefully Odysseus returned his eyes to deck, knowing
himself to be standing on splinters and seeing dead friends.

CXVIII.

"At last in cold resolve, he took a great heart-charging breath
and turned to face dread Scylla's terror inconceivable.
He squared his stance; his eyes began a slow painstaking search
up the wall, ready for any assault; no vagrant thought,
no word, could breach between controlling mind and quickened sense.
'There! High above the forehead of the cliff, the very crown,
an opening! Come out! Whatever you are, here am I!'"

CXIX.

Here Anamusa paused, slid back in her chair, raised her eyes
to the window above our loving configuration
and exhaled. A lightening flash, still fearsome in its beauty,
raised the darkness, held it up stretched and lit across the sky,
until a second burst came on, stronger still, almost the dawn.
"Do not relax yet, friends," she said firmly. Do not allow
the body's interval to claim the mind. Endure, endure."

CXX.

She turned her head right to Marco, who had planted his feet
firmly on the floor. He squared his shoulders and leaned forward,
poised to begin. "Dear friends, Marco's story is companion
to my own, two strands braided in a filament," she said.
"A double helix," he suggested. With the softest smile,
he turned his eyes to hers, as if to receive a blessing,
which her eyes granted; then returning, he began his tale.

End, Book Three

Book Four : *The Cross*

I.

"Having descended from the upper room into darkness,
Jesus led by single torch a few who would not leave him.
Over Cedron to Gethsemanee they moved, not knowing
what would come next or when, but mustering their readiness.
By the first olive, the tree of life, at the garden's edge,
Jesus stopped and spoke, 'I would enter here and pray alone.
Stay awake and watch. I will return with clear intention.'

II.

"About thirty paces did he move, found an open spot
and brought himself down, clumsily prostrate, to the hard ground.
'My Lord, speak loudly, for the tempter screams for me to run,
to save the life he understands. Not his but yours am I.
Offer me your cup and though my throat tighten with his lies
and my lower coils spasm and rebel, I will take it.
But do not wait. Do not defeat my heart's small attention.'

III.

"He returned to find his friends nodding, the torchlight mocking
their drooping heads. 'I judge you not, but if you would make use
of what is coming, you must watch, be ready, and fear not
great marvels and men hating you. Our life is not the world's.
You must expect to stand before the crowd as aliens
and not be disgraced. Indestructible prayers define us,
and we must pray even as people threaten and curse us.'

IV.

"' I am humbled, Lord,' said Peter. 'Why can't I stay awake?
When you depart, even a short space, my eyes grow heavy
and my neck bows as if to slip into a noose. What am I?'
'You are the willing of no will, a believer adrift
in a hungry sea,' said the master. 'A rope has been thrown
for you to cling to, but the ship does not tarry. Hold on.
Stay above the surface. Desperate must we be for truth.'

V.

"'Myself am not yet firm,' said Jesus softly. 'Watch and pray.'
He returned to his place of solitary prayer, his heart
kindling to flame, his rhythmic words asserting potency.
'My God, you have readied me. May you watch in glory now
as I face the mob and defend the path to your presence.'
And again he returned to his disciples and found them
chins on chest bones, and he roused them with great, merciful heart.

VI.

"Out of the darkness came a ragged, scuttling mob, closer
and closer, peppered with voices. Jesus, his torch aloft,
stood to confront them. And striding up to him, supported
by a gang of priests and beggars, came his lost student Judas,
who with his kiss on Jesus' cheek signaled the hostile crowd
to clench their circle round the master. Peter seized a sword,
but Jesus checked him. 'Surrender and all resistance drop.'

VII.

"The master sat in the cell, the mocking purple draped
upon him, bloodied from his lacerations, slimed with spit.
The rivulets of blood descending from his punctured scalp
had dried, matting his hair and crusting his face. He rested,
gathering himself to face the final brutality.
A thought came: 'Judas has lost the judgment. He is reclaimed
by what he had earlier forsaken. I will miss him.'

VIII.

"Knowing the kind agony Heaven had devised to be
inconceivable to him, in the occupier's jail
as a petty criminal he sat, a laughable prince
of fools to all below him, to all above a great king
whose sitting made his seat a throne. His strange quest of the truth
fed upon his fixed awareness of his battered senses
and fortified his choice to let God's conscious will unfold.

IX.

"Breath by breath he waited, the kite of his mind kept aloft
by the smallest shifting of his pain. This was holy time.
The concerns carried up to the gate of his attention
were politely turned away, except those of simplest strength.
First accept, then embrace: the lesson of transformation.
Return and again return: the lesson of building will.
To such fundamental principles was his life reduced.

X.

"And holding everything together – the blue-gray shadows,
the foul mustiness of his wounds, the unyielding cold stone
he sat upon, the greasy bitterness inside his mouth,
the crude noise of the crowd outside – unifying the world
and keeping his separate mind, were his ongoing prayers.
Even now, with sweet drowsiness leaning its healing weight
on his throbbing neck, he held the rhythm of attention.

XI.

"The rusty cell door opened with a wincing whine. Rough hands
dragged him up and out and down to the judgment hall again.
There Pilate waited, a politic man feeling the law
for a loophole. Sickened by the sight of the mocked master,
he moved to the balcony with a cynic's irony
to proclaim, 'Behold the man.' The obedient fury
of the crowd, led by the priests, demanded crucifixion.

XII.

"Then Jesus knew and accepted and embraced Heaven's price.
With a detectable quaver in his voice, Pilate asked,
'Knowest thou not I have the power to crucify thee
or release thee? Speak!' For the first time in hours, the master
gave his breath to worldly words. 'That which has delivered me
to you and now surrounds me with actors blind and blameless
screaming murder – that great love beyond wills what here must be.'

XIII.

"Pilate trembled and moved gravely to the balcony, knowing
he must give the mob its sacrifice, that such is the world.
He ordered an inscription made, to be placed on the cross:
'Jesus of Nazareth, King of the Jews." Hearing these words,
the priests objected, 'Say only that he calls himself so.'
Emerging from the hell of his own thoughts, Pilate answered,
'Let it be as I have said,' and he gave Jesus over.

XIV.

"They stripped him of the purple, replaced his own seamless robe,
and led him off, ordering Simon, a willing student,
to help his master carry the cross. To him Jesus spoke,
'Let not the pulse of the angry crowd determine your pace.
Walk on with intentional steps that your prayers be remembered.'
For this work Simon was granted a vision of the soul
of his master, undisturbed, separate from the body.

XV.

"Through the streets of the sacred city moved the hating crowd,
not knowing whence their hate, and the still mind of the master
at the center, for whom the jeers were as donkeys braying.
Past the gates toward the hill of the skull moved the procession,
the taunts closer and louder, the mockeries emboldened
by impunity. The master's eye discerned the faces
of the priests exhorting the crowd, urgent as in battle.

XVI.

"Swept along by the oppressive human wave, the master
marveled at the violence upheaving from each fellow.
In each contorted face he saw unfathomed fervor,
minds given over, organized to grim fatality.
He also felt within his bowels the pitiful part
that wanted with equal loss of mind to break and run,
to get away or be expunged in the mad rush of flight.

XVII.

"All this he contained in the rhythm of his steps, straining
but with each breath reclaiming certainty, remembering
highest Heaven watched his suffering and suffered with him.
At the foot of Golgotha, the seething mob hesitated
as if waiting on some strange permission. By priests dispatched,
three men clambered up the hill where between two nameless thieves
already hanging there, stood the stave meant for the master.

XVIII.

"They lifted it from its support and brought it to the ground,
and the crowd surged forward, shoving Jesus on. A hard kick
to the back of his knee dropped him to the dirt where rough hands
forced him on his back and stripped him. The cross piece Simon bore
was fitted into place, and the master roughly hoisted
over onto the cross. He watched the first nail pounded in
between his right wrist bones. Said Jesus, 'May it firmly hold.'

XIX.

"The pain of the first nail was bearable, though it worsened
as air entered the wound. He felt his left arm seized and stretched,
the hammering begun; with clear purpose and without haste,
his eyes moved to the painful noise: the second nail was in.
He knew then how death would come. His breath already struggled;
his chest so stretched, the air went only shallowly within.
Mindful of his breathing more than his pain, he watched the sky.

XX

"Only at the edges of the clouds could sunlight be seen.
The darkening pall extended. Many hands gripped his legs
and stretched them down until the sockets of his hips relaxed.
A small platform, a ledge, grazed his footsoles, not quite in reach
of his weight. Then both legs were forcibly turned to the right
and his ankles brought together bone on bone. The splinters
from the stave pierced the flesh of his right leg. He braced for pain.

XXI.

"And the pain came. First the hammer blow's clank, then instantly
within the vibrations of that impact surged the torment
as the spike, bigger than the other two, ripped through the flesh
just above the ankle bones and fastened in the stave wood.
He felt the cry explode deep within and burst from his mouth
unresisted, uncontrolled by his still separate mind.
His body was a stuck thing, bent, throbbing and distended.

XXII.

"He had held and was holding and would hold. He knew he could,
not by his own great will, though he would need its constancy,
but by the perfect calibrations of Heaven whose plan
gave pain only equal to the presence he could summon.
The crowd, now muttering low, paused with uncertain shuffling
and gave him space, while Jesus, clear in silence, understood
the flesh that he was not but that he must yet use till death.

XXIII.

"A centurion standing by signaled the eager priests
who in turn signaled their henchmen. Nine strong men gathered round
the cross and in unison raised it straight as a pillar,
fixing its foot in the permanent groove. Jesus' body
slid down and dangled, the ankle stake cutting through sinew
till the balls of his feet found the ledge to push against.
His shoulder sockets held, and little breaths moved in and out.

XXIV.

"Such was his stability, the pain a river flooding
through him he must not resist but let be, for fighting now
would only kill him sooner. In a slow conscious movement,
he raised his eyes. 'So this is how it is. So be it, Lord.'
The rude crowd milled around stupefied in dampened hatred.
Tasting blood, Jesus sought what his other senses offered,
and lest he faint, asserted within, 'My prayer is to feel.'

XXV.

"Against the blackening sky, the three crosses stood; the one
between gathered beneath it a small band of witnesses
in vigil, shivering at the sight. The thieves left and right
were lashed, not nailed, to their staves, and with effort yet could speak.
The larger crowd, fearful of the sky or ignorant now
of how to feel or what to do, drained away; suffering
united the rest. Jesus found his mother there below.

XVI.

"Responding to his gaze, she spoke. 'My son, is this the end?
When you were four years old, you warned me you would break my heart.
I could not understand you, but I knew from your strange birth
that your return to God would be abandonment, a wound
that even now is tearing. I hoped to die before you,
to be spared this witnessing, but I followed your teaching,
submitted to the prayers, and now must watch your agony.'

XXVII.

"He gazed at her with eyes that were as brimming pools of love.
Beside her on the right, young John, faithful and beloved,
had moved in support. She laid her head on his soft shoulder.
The comely disciple then found his Lord's eyes and knew him.
He spoke with quavering voice, 'Master, help me understand this.'
Jesus gathered breath and spoke, 'Make ready those who follow.
Woman, behold thy son.' And to John, 'Behold thy mother.'

XXVIII.

"Suddenly from the master's left came rude, cackling laughter.
'What a joke this is, to laugh my last few breaths away!
The king prepares for his succession as his execution
takes its course. What heart! How responsible can a man be?
You bleed and suffocate yet think yourself upon a throne.
We others are merely dying.' Mixed laughter and coughing
followed from the thief. 'No end to mockery,' whispered John.

XXIX.

"But from the right the other thief now spoke, 'I merely die,
as you say, but he is using dying. I think I see.
Each breath he takes is an intention. He is not yet throned
but mounting, and death will crown him. What mystery is this?
From your kingdom, remember me.' Jesus turned with care,
'And thyself remember, friend, so as to follow me home.'
In wonder John and Mary received their understanding.

XXX.

"A priest spoke up at Jesus with disdain, 'If you are king,
order your servants to rescue you from your affliction.
What king is this who rots stretched on a cross in infamy?'
He spat to punctuate his poisoned words. Not looking down,
Jesus grasped and released three breaths, and with the fourth he prayed,
'Father, I would finish this task. I see its beauty now.
Opposing words rise in me. To their dungeon send them back.'

XXXI.

"'What will break first,' said the caustic thief, 'his gut or his heart?'
'We barely draw breath,' said the other. 'He gasps but to pray.'
'My Lord,' said John 'some nepenthe. Let me soak a new cloth
and bring it to your lips. Heaven wants not this agony.'
'No, my boy,' said Jesus softly. 'When I need it, I will ask.
As long as my mind is in control, I would bear the pain.
You and the angels watching know the greater suffering.'

XXXII.

"'Did you hear, comrade?' the bitter thief laughed and groaned at once.
'He pities Heaven. Such words take vanity to madness.
There is no Heaven, King of Fools. Any God worth your prayers
would not amuse himself with torture. The sky is empty,
or peopled with fiends. This crucified man has come unhinged.'
'I know otherwise,' said John. 'You cannot see your own nose.'
'Be still,' said Jesus straining. 'Who profits from your reply?'

XXXIII.

"'You envy him. I see it now,' said the clear-sighted thief.
'He has something you cannot have, and you'd mock him for it.
For him death is a destination, for you a terror.'
John then spoke in soft contrition. 'My anger serves nothing.
It is more food for your devouring irony. O man,
this close to your end, will you not surrender and have peace?'
'You're an elegant boy,' said the thief. 'Stay with your mother.'

XXXIV.

"There followed some minutes of no speech as each adjusted
to the rate of dying and bargained with its pressing force.
The grim thief wondered if by any whore he'd made a son.
The young thief softly wept, wondering if his mother lived.
Mary forced her eyes to see her son and her lips to form prayers.
John knew a heart of weighty helplessness but did not shrink.
Jesus watched the sky, overfull of molten clouds and dust.

XXXV.

"He looked out over Jerusalem, now darkened out of time.
He saw the great temple burning to the ground, in his ears
the death cries above the roar of flames. A sharp, jabbing pain
from his twisted lower spine called him back, but he released
his mind from its hot clutch and reopened to his vision.
He felt the heat move over him, his feet on burning stone,
and soldiers running wild, their blades ripping bodies like fruit.

XXXVI.

"The blood in the street ran as if it had rained from the sky.
A horse with mounted warrior charged directly, coming,
thundering, but what insignia on the rider's shield?
Not Roman, no….but a cross! 'The slaughter's symbol changes
but the slaughter goes on. Jerusalem, Jerusalem,
whoreslave of religion, how often must you be destroyed?'
Jesus dropped his eyes. 'Father, I have felt what man can feel.'

XXXVII.

"Hearing these faint words, John moved closer. They met eye to eye.
'John, my son, let not my teaching be a mere religion.
Belief is not enough, nor hope, to keep the mind in God.'
'As you say, Master. I will remember, as I do now.'
And John found the rhythm of his prayer within and looked up
to a sky whose ghostly clouds rolled and roiled, mocking the sun.
He was unmoved by nature's gloom and continued his prayer.

XXXVIII.

"Four soldiers stood below the cross, like patient vultures fixed
on a downed animal soon to die. One declared desire
for the Master's seamless robe, but his claim was contested
by the others, each of whom thought the garment rightly his.
Back and forth they bickered, their thick voices joined in jabber.
At last the most grizzled one raised his arms to still the noise:
'We all have our claims. Selfishness moves reason. Let's cast lots.'

XXXIX.

"And down they crouched, four men before the Lord they did not know,
vying for the seamless robe they coveted, throwing bones.
Their voices grew louder as they fixed on the game, deafened
to all else, oblivious, focused on a gambler's chance.
John observed them thinking, 'Even some of the Master's students
would join in that game, desiring the Master's robe. Here is man,
forsaking true instruction to play at bones in the dark.'

XL.

"Barely audible were Jesus' words from the cross, 'I thirst.'
John moved to the soldier in charge and asked that drink be brought,
but one that had earlier mocked the master took poor wine
from his own bundle and soaked a sponge cloth in it.
Another brought a reed to lift the cloth to Jesus' mouth.
The master moved his lips as if to kiss and sucked the wine
to wash the tongue and free the voice for final utterance.

XLI.

"And then arose the winner of the bone game, exulting,
holding the master's garment high and taunting his companions.
Seeing this display, Jesus willed the air into his chest
and said, 'Father, forgive them, for they know not what they do,'
and Mary through her tears replied, 'Forgive, forgive, forgive.'
Then a soft chant started up from the Master's mouth, shocking
those who heard. 'My God, my God, why have you forsaken me?'

XLII.

"But John alone understood and comforted his mother.
'Even now, he prays the psalm.' The chant faded into air,
became inaudible, though the Master's lips continued
movements barely seen. At last, John stepped forth to intervene,
saying, 'They shall come, and shall declare his righteousness
unto a people that shall be born, that he hath done this.'
The psalm closed, Jesus mouthed the words, 'It is finished. Let be.'

XLIII.

"His eyes rolled over to the right, his head sank to his chest,
his torso slackened, and a draft of air whispered forth.
So witnessed Mary and John, but the Master knew himself
as if under water in a cave, rising by levels,
and on each level demons he had known from his own flesh
brandishing their blades and threatening. Upward he traveled,
past inmost devils impotently hissing for belief.

XLIV.

"The dangling body collapsed against the cross, and the wrists,
bearing the full weight, began to tear and bleed and crumble.
The Master continued his ascent, maintaining presence
as the light of his being rose out of the gut of hell,
past the portal of patience to the chamber of the heart,
past the throat no longer strangled by wads of rotting words,
past the eyes no longer veiled by the mind's indulgent screen.

XLV.

"Though having watched the complete passion, John and Mary stood
in shock before the heaping body, past words and past tears.
At last John summoned himself and said, 'Let us not leave him
hanging here as criminal flesh. Give him just burial.
Clean him, bathe his hair in precious unguent, resolve his wounds,
anoint and pacify his face. Respect this brave vessel
which bore the words of higher worlds to us here ignorant.'

XLVI.

"Just then the commanding soldier did his wretched duty,
stabbing the point of his spear into the body's right breast.
And the conscious spirit within was aware of a noise
and a percussion from below, itself having entered
the great horn whose mouthpiece in the center of the forehead
extends and widens to the crown of the head and beyond,
out of time and space to the light, which is eternity.

XLVII.

"There moving through the shaft, open, thus illuminated,
the spirit visited again the elevated states
which had trained stubborn flesh and fed higher aspirations.
Down this shaft, entering as terror, exiting as love,
had come the revelations taught to him by all prophets.
As back up the shaft the spirit rose, the brightening light
and states less comprehensible pushed presence to bursting.

XLVIII.

"And then emergence! Out from the crown of the lifeless skull
into the light no longer veiled, up through the thinning air,
rising faster than all sense of speed, the gross atmosphere
of earth left behind like water by a finished bather.
But who is this beside? Another presence, form of light.
Joseph! Awakener! Clear at last from tiny earth,
the two beings knew each other in effulgent silence.

XLIX.

"What can pass between two angels passed between them, their love
unalloyed, their knowledge instantaneous. Who on earth
had been Hebrew lord of Egypt, and the Jew beyond Jews
now shared in Heaven's harmony the fruits of their being:
embrace electric and illuminate, unbarred passage
of all of each into the other, pure magnetic bliss
of mutual honor culminating mystic ages.

L.

"From his guide, Jesus absorbed gratitude for the great line
of prophets preceding him – Abraham, Isaac, Jacob –
all completed men now sharing the universe in God;
and homage to Egypt, fount of liberating knowledge
in enduring form, whose childlike art preserves the secrets
of deathless identity for all succeeding Schoolmen
of this Great Age, the spells that hover on the breath of life.

LI.

"And from Awakened to Awakener: also great thanks,
for guidance birth to death, for holding the perfect present,
keeping it accessible through every earthly error,
nursing budding consciousness by patient overwatching;
and as well to Egypt praise for knowledge learned on sojourn
that allowed the Hebrew Scriptures to come clear, their secrets
lost to cultural obedience, retrieved in glory.

LII.

"And both in simultaneous praise remembered Moses,
the great bridge between Mother Egypt and her Hebrew child,
he of great error and greater penitence, who carried
a School within him and, gifted face to face by God,
re-established civilization. There in the rapport
of eternity, the two merged honoring him whose face
in later earthly life had early Heaven's radiance.

LIII.

"And on the portal Moses opened, both meditated:
how many now residing out of time had come through it,
prophets and warriors in procession. There was David,
who had no rest from the sword but whose great songs are complete;
and Solomon, unparalleled in wisdom; and a line
of warners, their minds burned holy by the fire of God's voice –
Elijah, Isaiah, Jeremiah, Ezekiel.

LIV.

"And there between our praising pair, as if touched and summoned
by their love, came Moses himself, perfect in radiance.
What had been two were now three, and their great affinity
held them as they shared a presence multiplied in glory.
So unified of being were they in contemplation
that all Heaven registered in simplest felicity
their concord, the planets aware in conscious silence.

LV.

"And they all marveled at the progress that had fashioned them,
spirit's counterflow, the movement back and up the great ray,
opposing dying matter's mindless descent to cold ash.
And at once in them formed cognizance we would hear as words:
know the being we partake in is God and only God;
and our living is returning to God and only God;
by love to love ascending, loving God and only God.

LVI.

"In the reined ecstasy which was their respiration,
wordless they wondered at the design nearly completed.
From Abraham to Jesus was a line, one strand of God,
and the seal of prophets, of all warners the most steadfast,
the messenger Muhammad, yet to come. And from each point,
each figure on the line, extended further strands to saints
and seers, all connected, one of the great nets of an Age.

LVII.

"And to each Age – before whose dim beginning man's memory
could not travel but was confounded by fragments of facts –
were many nets, some large, some larger, to bring home the souls
in prodigal return over lifetimes of relearning.
And as the Age concluded, and the earth required respite,
one would come to stitch the nets together and make them whole,
manifest their hidden harmony brought aboard one ship.

LVIII.

"But he who would captain the conscious bark they could not see.
Contemplating there together, Joseph, Moses, Jesus
felt an end, an opacity of vision, the design
dimming before completion. Why could they not know this one,
whom we, seven friends gathered on their way home to wait out
an ominous storm, have the honor to know and attend?
They know him now, as we do, and their net has been retrieved.

LIX.

"But then in wisdom of their limits they knew not to grope,
not to resist, not to reach for what was not yet revealed.
Three as one, they allowed their contemplation to relax
in knowing that a new labor would come clear before them.
From the greater light above them coalesced a presence
of shocking being: Archangel Michael, who lives witness
to the unbearable light of God's own face, now appeared.

LX.

"Not without honored suffering, the three prophets welcomed
with their fused attention the Absolute's emissary,
and the four were as one in will and loving delight.
With tenderness restraining awful strength, like a father
lifting up a newborn son, Michael focused his being
onto Jesus, as the others beside him in support
and the attendant universe cherished ready silence.

LXI.

"In the communion of Heaven, Michael made the message
he'd been sent to give present to Jesus, suffusing him
with a will transcending his own, and Jesus understood.
What in immediate perfection passed between these two
to make them one in will, we can only know by poor words,
God's most abused blessing, given to man to use in praise
of God and our return to him, but wasted in chatter.

LXII.

"For our minds, here is Michael's message, which Jesus obeyed.
'The intimations given you while still in flesh were true,
even as you told them to your students. You must return,
though only briefly, to complete the building of your way.
They must know you transcended – they will say 'resurrected'.
You must appear in flesh a while longer, putting it on
and taking it off, that your students know you are not flesh.

LXIII.

"'Seeing you thus, and touching you, they will have certainty
of what is possible for them. Only then will they make
sufficient sacrifice to burn with fired attention
the past and future from the mind, and to protect the heart,
and keep its upward longing free from downward folly.
Forty earth days you must keep with them, thirty and then ten,
even as Moses did before seeing God face to face.

LXIV.

"'This task is not without danger, not without suffering.
Make pact with me. Through my mind God affirms your loyalty,
and upon your return, face to face. Beloved fellows
bolstering him with love, do not let him miscalculate
the painful grip of flesh, that neither at top nor bottom
of the spine he allow himself to be fully taken.
Throat and rectum, high and low, strangle the light of the soul.'

LXV.

"With this strange remonstrance Michael ended; though Jesus knew
these things, he was touched by the reminding. The archangel
gave a careful bow, and Jesus knew that any gesture
of more merger, any fuller fusion, would make re-entry
greater agony. He turned to Moses, who offered him
a half-embrace, and with it a wondrous bliss of being
that he dared not yet delight in and could not yet return.

LXVI.

"Then Joseph, the Awakener, who had been with Jesus
since his conscious seed arrived to fill Mary's perfect womb,
enwrapped his charge in loving farewell. Together as one
with his guide, Jesus understood that all had been given.
This last task would be his own, for those ascending through him.
In no measure of time, the four held their sweet conference
and let abide the full being known only in silence.

LXVII.

"When Michael turned to ascend, as if in compensation
Jesus felt the touch of gravity, the beginning downward
which he did not resist. Through the ethers he descended,
holding himself clear-purposed; permitting no sensation
to become disruption, his awareness of attention,
which is truth, remained unbroken. He gave his whole being
to guarding presence, letting Heaven have its way with him.

LXVIII.

"Then there he was, observing his former body below,
the crypt illuminated by the light of consciousness.
Moving inevitably back to his unquickened flesh,
he was given a brief flash of knowing what awaited:
of rediscovering daylight, and feet against the earth,
of traveling to regather and reunite the will
of his students, now shocked, disoriented and confused.

LXIX.

"Then into the calm corpse he moved, entering at the crown,
and down the shaft to the holy window between the eyes,
the balcony of love, the last perch of conscious freedom
before burial in the already buried body.
The firings in the cold brain commenced, accelerating,
and he knew his eyes, yet unopened, and the thick scent
of fetid air moving into him, inflating his lungs.

LXX.

"And with sudden seismic pounding, like a deep earthquake,
his great heart resumed its work, and the rest of the human
responded, as from frozen winter beckoned by the sun.
Yet still down he traveled, to the sinuous putrid halls
of corruption, where he confronted in clear victory
the carnal king, the lower self in its lair, shocked to life,
captured in fear, without plan, and knowing itself mastered.

LXXI.

"Then up again he traveled, through the patience gate, to give
presence to the heart, abide with it in common purpose
and restore the meaning to its brave consistent labor;
thence up again through the throat held open in submission
to the balcony of love and the sun disk throne behind
and above—the two placements from which the married spirit
rules the body—he spread himself in sentiency throughout.

LXXII.

"His eyes opened and a great pervasive pain erupted
from the corridors of sense, a wave to ride or drown in.
He felt the grip of the revived emboldened liar close
high and low on his spine. 'Release your hold,' he said in mind.
Could he walk? What the task of Heaven requires, he reasoned,
Heaven makes provision for. 'Let my shoulder find the stone,
and let the unveiled light return to bless what I must be.'

LXXIII.

Here Marco stopped. The patterned breathing of his listeners
merged in common exhalation as the first flush of dawn
appeared in the window. Each one held the cherished silence
as if nursing a babe in arms. The long night was over,
though the work, for which the heart was now refreshed, was the same.
Around our loving company, the groggy mass bestirred
but did not wake, resisting till required the coming sun.

LXXIV.

Carroll at last declared in praise, "What a transparent pair
of tales you have told. Our purpose now is plain to complete.
You called the first two stories the pillars of our temple;
then you, Ana, dressed our temple's inner court with its theme.
And Marco, mindful of how far we'd come, designed a tale
preserving our progress, bridging the night, and making clear
the bright distinction of our state. Do you see our prize, friends?"

LXXV.

Jules spoke in reply, his lips upturned in a knowing smile,
"We've passed the night in prayer, with two more prayers yet unoffered."
"Exactly," said Carroll. "Now more conscious of our effort,
we must complete the task in artistry obedient."
"Yes, I see," said Mathilde. "What I began in good faith
has become a greater thing, elevating all of us.
Ruby's tale must now fulfill a place in the procession."

LXXVI.

"I don't understand what you mean," said Ruby. "It's my turn,
that I know, but what new obligation must I fulfill?"
Here I confess that I was equally befuddled,
and Ruby and I were sudden comrades in confusion.
Carroll looked carefully at Anamusa whose deep eyes
were wells of parental compassion. He then turned to Jules,
then to Marco and Mathilde, receiving accord from each.

LXXVII.

Finally, after acknowledging me and pointing high
the index finger of his right hand, he turned his kind face
to Ruby and spoke with the gentleness of a father.
"We've discovered ourselves in the middle of a sequence
of prayers, my dear, and that discovery has begotten
the aim to finish that design more intentionally.
We hope you can give us a tale advancing our sequence."

LXXVIII.

Ruby's eyes still had the light glaze of incoherent thoughts,
and her shoulders hunched to bear the pressure of performance.
I waited for the explanation I was sure would come,
knowing the others as I did; it was Jules who began.
"Ruby, please be at peace. We will explain. Whatever time
and help you need to fit your tale to our newfound purpose,
we pledge, wanting not a contest but a choir's harmony."

LXXIX.

Reassured, Ruby replied, "I'm long enough in this School
to know to expect abrupt change, so I will not resist;
but I also know best efforts follow understanding,
and at this moment I don't understand what's happened.
Apparently Ana and Marco offered us something
in their tales that has changed the whole complexion of our game."
I too was pressed to wonder what our game had now become.

LXXX.

Mathilde spoke with benevolent softness. "When I began
my tale, I had in mind to represent the unspoiled heart's
search for the miraculous. We all embarked on that search,
and what we passed through, I tried to show in simple symbols
dressed in childlike humor. The path to School, if we are blessed
ever to find School, is circuitous and mystical,
and I wanted to recall the flavor of it for us."

LXXXI.

"And well you did," acknowledged Ruby, the others adding
their approval. "My own path came not through a magic forest
but through a desert," Ruby noted, but the atmosphere
was wondrous and charmed with just enough strange difficulty.
The feeling of being led was always there, though head bumps
and stubbed toes were plentiful. The weird dream that closed your tale
stumped me, but now it seems a final payment for the truth."

LXXXII.

'Yes," said Mathilde, "a willing split from the known must be made."
"One discovers oneself in the unknown," Marco added,
"but when the Gods offer the gift of a School, they present
enough of the higher world, enough mystical events,
so that one is choosing between strange life and certain death.
"So Jules," Ruby noted, "your story began as a tribute
to Mr. Andersen. How did it become so much more?"

LXXXIII.

Jules shifted in his seat wondering if he could explain
the growth of his story. "We've all had the experience
of the Gods putting words in our mouths, of utterances
that surprised us with their truth but which never had been thought
before they were spoken. By the time the princess appeared
in my story, it was my story no longer. The Gods
carried the narrative until I could catch up with them."

LXXXIV.

"And how do you see what was made?" Ruby asked carefully.
Jules composed himself a moment then spoke with certainty
and sweet solemnity. "It is the story of a man
awakening and founding a School, first within himself
and then in the world. From the mystical marriage that closed
the tale, a higher order can come forth, and for a time
a society of Heavenly striving can here exist."

LXXXV.

A long moment of silence followed. We were all
becoming aware of what was emerging from our work.
At last Ruby spoke. "So the first two tales are the pillars
of the temple; it's not just Anamusa'a metaphor.
Without quite knowing it, we committed ourselves to build
a sacred structure, a prayer sequence as a story round.
The first two steps are a promise to God that we're coming."

LXXXVI.

"And a promise to ourselves," said Ana, smiling brightly.
"And so your awe at Jules' story, your own trepidation,
and your collaboration with Marco were the results
of seeing where we were going," Carroll said. "Thank you both."
"Yes, thank you, but what theme have you given us?" asked Ruby.
"If I'm to follow you, I must understand precisely
how your tales have advanced us and what the next step must be."

LXXXVII.

Ana began her explanation. "Marco understood
immediately what I revealed and that a great theme
was required. In our prayer, the theme, or third step, is a bold thrust
of attention specific to one sense, a firm command
that will bear repeating later; and the fourth step is a bridge,
a retrospective and reaffirmation of the goal.
The fifth step, where we are now, echoes and confirms the third.

LXXXVIII.

"And in deciding a theme, I wished to extend the thread
that had appeared – the search for truth – then the awakening
of a young master and his establishment of a School.
What had been our third phase after our naïve beginning
and our long foundation? You'll recall, we lived a decade
with the Greeks, imbibing their spirit and their high knowledge.
It seemed fitting that my theme would ride on a Greek tale."

LXXXIX.

"To follow Prince Plato!" Ruby beamed in epiphany.
"Yes, that helped," said Ana. "Jules, how did that name come to you?"
Jules smiled with humility as he pointed to the sky.
Again and again we discover the Gods," said Mathilde.
"For they are always with us," Carroll added, "revealing
themselves for our discovery, even now." Then Jules chimed,
"They reside in the present, calling us; we come and go."

XC.

Ana continued, "It was here that Marco and I had our long chat.
Something he said started a chain of association
that ended in the recognition of a likely theme.
"Tell us, Marco," said Jules. Marco spoke deliberately.
"I observed to Ana that all human life seemed to transpire
in only three states: presence, the striving after presence
and its prolonging, or its loss to unmindfulness."

XCI.

Marco expounded, "Prolonged presence we may call divine,
and we cherish it above all. Striving after presence
is the work of what we call the steward, that part of us
conceived and nourished by School work, the intelligent heart
educated in ancient knowledge. Last, the brute mortal
living for its appetites, the instinctive element
to which we descend in tragic thrall so much of the time."

XCII.

"Of these things it's ever good to be reminded, " said Jules.
"And the stories we take inspiration from," said Ana
"are those of striving – some embodiment of the steward
laboring for transcendence. Epic poems, sacred texts –
in the greatest stories, we watch a heroic figure
helped by Heaven, battle the lower chaos in himself.
What he strives for is divine, what he strives against is dead."

XCIII.

"Dead?" asked Ruby. "Dead in the sense of unconscious, wanting
only the security of earthbound things," said Ana.
"So you chose the steward's struggle as your theme," said Carroll.
"Our struggle. On the internal scale of the prayer sequence,
we are the steward, but on the scale of sacred stories
we observe him as the hero, his higher consciousness
betokened by his divine favor and communication."

XCIV.

"But I thought Odysseus was only seeking wife and home.
Could a goal be more instinctive than that?" Ruby challenged.
"Wife and home are symbols," said Ana firmly. "All tales
of the steward are symbolic, though often regarded
as historical by the cultures that hold them sacred.
Home is the state of presence to which he is returning –
in the end in full ownership – by transforming suffering."

XCV.

"And the coupling in the great bed strapped to the olive tree
represents the final marriage of higher elements,
the male and the female – by which transcendent consciousness
is crystallized," said Marco. "The marriage of higher parts
is another frequent theme in such works, but Ana chose
an episode symbolic of the internal struggle
with imagination – the Siren voices always here."

XCVI.

After moments of silence fixing her thoughts, Ruby asked,
"So Homer's poem is an epic work on consciousness,
an allegory of awakening?" "Yes," said Ana.
"And of course more," interjected Carroll. "It operates
on many levels. I call it a foundation poem
to differentiate it from a sacred text, but all
such terms reveal the intellect's too clever self-delight."

XCVII.

"Was it a product of a School?" Ruby asked. "I'm not sure.
There's sure indication of the sacred keys, and Homer
understood the higher meaning of the materials
he inherited, and built a great hall to house a new
flowering of civilization," said Carroll. "His work
and others like it – maps of consciousness – were what our School
needed in its adolescence, before the keys appeared."

XCVIII.

"Actually," said Ana, "I see keys in Homer's work,
but to me they feel less vital, more eroded by time.
Odysseus strapped to the mast resembles Christ on the cross,
but it is less definite, and the text less developed.
"As you might have guessed," said Marco, "their similarity
sparked my story, and there are other Homeric echoes
in the Gospels; for instance, the cleansing of the temple."

XCIX.

"Let us not indulge intellectual vanity, friends.
Speculation will not long support presence," warned Mathilde.
"Thank you, Mathilde. You are right," said Ruby, "but may we go
just a little further until I understand the way
my story must connect to those already told?" We looked
at each other, made a silent agreement, firmed our grips
on the present, and signaled Ruby of our readiness.

C.

"Now are you saying," Ruby continued relentlessly,
that the Gospel writers knew their Homer?" We all waited
until Marco spoke with a deliberate calming tone.
"It's possible. Homer's place in the Greco-Roman world
was such that most educated men were versed in his works,
and the Evangelists were not uneducated men.
But the Christ story draws from other traditions as well."

CI.

"Christ is an esoteric hero," Marco continued,
"as was Horus and Moses and Mithras. The Christ story
is a grand synthesis in which are seen the great heroes
of the Mediterranean past, and in which the keys
of conscious life are hidden. An instructed man will find
therein the same permanent principles of transcendence
as can be found in sacred texts from Egypt to Tibet."

CII.

"What you say is not unknown to me," Ruby admitted,
"but my study is just beginning." Carroll intervened,
"It may be better to think of the theme of our sequence
of stories as the heroes of the one great tradition,
the work of Conscious School on earth. The manifestations
are many, some closer to the vital line than others,
each wearing the particular costume of a culture."

CIII.

"It is perilously easy to believe our knowledge
is our being. I suggest we straighten ourselves to task
lest we lose presence to vanity of mind," said Mathilde.
"She is right," said Jules. "Worldly knowledge is an allurement,
and it is a short step from speculation to belief."
"Let me ask one very specific question," said Ruby.
"How precisely are the masters of the mast and cross the same?"

CIV.

"Not the same, but analogous," answered Anamusa..
"Odysseus strapped to the mast battles imagination,
wandering mind, and winning in that instance, is granted
a vision, a higher understanding. His suffering
on the mast and later between Scylla and Charibdis
is the cost, which he pays willingly. He is a hero
of consciousness, a steward we say, mastering himself."

CV.

Anamusa continued, "But Christ on the cross portrays
the ancient posture more precisely, just as the true keys
are more than mere metaphors. His arms extended signal
the completion of the prayer sequence, just as in Egypt.
But Marco's daring story went further, dramatizing
the prayer sequence and the Heavenly silences beyond.
I hope you found the beauty." She finished and was silent.

CVI.

As were we all for some moments. The earliest sunlight
was trickling around the thinning clouds and down through the windows.
The terminal was stirring and mumbling in the last throes
of sleep. At last Carroll spoke, "I did detect it, Marco –
the rhythm of the sequence in your tale. Didn't we all?"
"I confess I did not," said Ruby, 'but I did wonder
about the after death passages, the great silences."

CVII.

"Yes," I said. "I too did not understand till the silences,
but I remember the story well enough to write it."
"Perhaps, William," said Jules, "when you see it on paper
beneath your pen, it will be clear to you. "Often," I said
with a smile, "that's the only time things are clear to me."
"Telling and writing tales," said Mathilde, "is one way to turn
inchoate experience into reminders of God."

CVIII.

"And now it is your turn, Ruby, " said Carroll. "By the time
you're done, the dawn will have delighted us and thoughts of home
will be prominent in our minds." "True, Carroll," Ruby said,
but something tells me that Heaven will have us waiting here
until your tale is told. If the story round we're making
is in fact a prayer sequence on a larger scale, I doubt
we'll be departing here until we have completed it."

CIX.

"You're likely right," said Carroll, somewhat chagrined, "We've just passed
through the interval and must not stop till finished in faith."
"Let me review what my place would have me do," said Ruby.
"I am to tell a tale of an esoteric hero,
one from a sacred text or from a foundation poem,
as Carroll calls it, and as mine is fifth in the sequence,
it must reiterate the theme of the mast or the cross."

CX.

"May I suggest," said Carroll, "the story of Osiris
trapped in the trunk of a tree, which after all might be
the source tale for this theme? An Egyptian steward story,
could we do better?" Ruby thought a moment then replied,
"It is a good suggestion, Carroll, but I'm the wrong tool.
Not having studied Egypt as I should, my mind finds there
nothing hospitable to this task. I must look elsewhere."

CXI.

"She's leaving Egypt to you, Carroll," Jules chimed, 'the sixth step."
"O my!" said Carroll. "Now I must rearrange my thinking."
"Yes, even as I am doing," said Ruby. "A question
remains about your story, Marco. As I understand
the prayer sequence, you weren't required to further Ana's theme.
Why did you do so?" "Truly, Ruby," Marco said simply,
"the story came to mind before its real purpose appeared."

CXII.

"Please explain," requested Ruby. Marco smiled happily.
"Ana told me of her tale, and the Christ story followed
effortlessly in my mind. I believe they are related,
that the four Evangelists were aware of their forebears,
but that's another matter. As the sequence was now clear,
the task of my place was to re-establish full presence,
penetrate any sleepiness veiling our real aim."

CXIII.

"And I thought we were just telling stories," marveled Ruby.
"We awake, awake and awake," said Mathilde most humbly.
"That is true," said Ruby, "and I have one last unveiling
to complete on this topic. Indulge me with your patience."
After moving her gaze from face to face, she continued,
"Just how, Marco, did your tale accomplish the backward look
the fourth step of the sequence requires? What am I missing?"

CXIV.

"You are right to ask, Ruby," Marco said. "The images
portraying the sequence, from the six men holding the rope
in the relief from Saqara to the sculpted ladder
on the Bath cathedral tower, do often dramatize
the fourth figure looking back, firming what has come before,
consolidating the prayer. We were mindful of the need
to include this element somehow." "Just how?" Ruby asked.

CXV.

"If you look at the tales told by Mathilde, Jules, and Ana,
all began with a preface, a conversation that moved
our focus to the story. But mine had no such prelude;
rather, we're discussing it now, in careful aftermath.
Carroll's eyebrows rose over widening eyes and a smile
bloomed on Jules' face as Marco continued, "The fourth story
reverses the established order and snaps the mind back."

CXVI.

"Now we find ourselves," Jules added, "in a state most unlike
our naïve beginning. A substantial offering presents
itself to be completed, and true conscience is alive."
"So you have told me, and truly I see it," said Ruby.
"Then you have a tale in mind?" Marco asked. "I have a thought
of a tale," Ruby allowed, "but inveterate self-doubt
is marshalling its forces. My feet aren't firm on this ground."

CXVII.

"We will help you, Ruby," Mathilde promised. "In recent years,
we've versed ourselves in sacred texts, which our sweet instruction
let us read as esoteric symbols breathing meaning."
"Yes, " said Carroll, "if you locate a tale from any one
of the great traditions, we can likely help you shape it."
"Carroll may exaggerate," Anamusa kindly said,
"but the task is ours, not merely yours, now that we see it."

CXVIII.

"What one learns, all learn," said Mathilde, "and we all know the work."
"So be it," Ruby said. "I seem to remember a part
in the Gilgamesh epic that echoes the noble theme
that Ana and Marco have offered us." Sudden silence,
the silence of surprise, came over the whole gathering.
Eyes widened and mouths fell slightly open. "What's the matter?"
Is that not appropriate?" Ruby asked delicately.

CXIX.

"It could not be more appropriate," Marco said at last.
"Forgive us, Ruby. It's the last thing we expected
to hear from you. We are embarrassed by our own surprise."
"I see," said Ruby, "you wonder how a black American
soldier girl knows the Gilgamesh story. I will explain.
It's not the mystery it may appear. Soldiers have time
to read, especially injured soldiers waiting to heal.

CXX.

The dawn was poised to enter the door of day, though the sun
had not yet come to open it. The terminal sleepers
were grudgingly surrendering to the aching advance
of wakefulness. Our little body, its task clarified
and conviction renewed, readied itself for the fifth tale,
the fifth step in our self-discovery. Evident now
was the mind of Heaven in each syllable we offered.

End, Book Four

Book Five: *The Sail*

I.

"How I came to be wounded is a hideous story,
so I will not protract it," Ruby said. "The healing days
are the important part—days of learning and decision."
So Ruby began, full-throated, calm; her voice issuing
like a jet of clear water belied her compact figure.
We sat startled by her strength. The newest child no longer,
she fixed us with her presence and the might of her address.

II.

"I fought in the useless war, the stupid, profligate war
that sealed our decline as a moral nation. I'm ashamed
of volunteering. I should have just retired, stepped away
from the unthinkable adventure, but the extra pay
seduced me. A down payment on a house I counted it,
the beginning of an after-Army life. Remember
we all thought it would be over in a handful of months.

III.

"So we went to the desert again to finish the job,
and the first few months were a cakewalk, a parade, a march
of unobstructed conquest. We did not know how deeply
in imagination was our victory. Baghdad fell
like a rotten tree, and we dreamed of the heroes' greetings
soon to come at home. It took a tedious year to glimpse
the truth, our self-importance stubborn in the blowing sand.

IV.

"So there I was still in the desert a full year later,
on endless patrols of vital road, riding with green kids
in a bulky vehicle we thought was safe. On a day
like any other, as we drove on another blank stretch,
a strange, alarming sight presented itself sixty yards
out in the sand: a child, a boy of seven or eight years,
tied to a flat rock as if waiting for Abraham's blade.

V.

"I ordered the driver, a boy who seemed not much older,
to stop, and I left the vehicle to investigate.
As I approached, I saw a strange smile distort the child's face.
I freed him with my knife, and he sat up but did not run,
his eerie smile taking on a cold, clutching constancy.
I freed myself from his gaze and had walked twenty yards back
when the rocket grenade hit our humvee and exploded.

VI.

"The shrapnel came at me like a swarm of hornets, pelting
and stinging me everywhere. I did not lose consciousness.
I stayed on my feet. A hit on the brow close my right eye,
But with my left I saw our humvee burn, the flames and smoke
taking what was left of my dismembered, blackened comrades.
It took a dozen surgeries to clean the metal out—
Baghdad, then Germany, then home. So my new life began.

VII.

"I turned thirty-eight in a hospital bed in a suburb
of D.C.; five months later, I retired from the Army.
I was both old and new, scarred but capable, rotted out
on duty and sick of soldiering, but empty and clean
for some new part—the rest of my life, yet undiscovered.
I needed to examine myself, explore the meaning
of my ongoing breathing. I wanted to be truthful.

VIII.

"Most of my race goes to church for consolation—not me.
Too many men out of their minds with passionate belief
in God and duty had blasted their way into my head,
my memory, for me to trust belief in anything.
And belief is the cost of consolation. Surrender
to belief and the whore, false comfort, comes to service you.
Excuse me. I'm too harsh. Sentimental types need belief.

IX.

"I needed clear sightedness because I wanted a truth
to ennoble my remaining years, a truth to become.
I had no idea how to search, no trust in advice,
just a tiny urgency, a persistent pilot light
to keep my mind remembering the aim. I found myself
more often in bookstores and libraries, not the searching
I'd imagined, but neither was I what I'd imagined.

X.

"The first book that penetrated deeply—I'm not ashamed—
was for children, a much shortened illustrated version
of *Don Quixote*. This fellow was mad, but his madness
was a mirror for mankind, stuck far out in make believe
trying to change what we misperceive. I laughed at the fool
until I got the joke the author was playing on me.
This man Miguel Cervantes was someone I could learn from.

XI.

"And when I read how he'd been a soldier shot in battle
against the Muslims and had spent years in prison, risking
his life many times trying to escape, my love for him
increased, and the flame of my aim became hot and more real.
Later, when I came to our School and discovered him here
among the enlightened men that we revere, I was glad
and thankful even for the children's version of his help.

XII.

"After the taste of Cervantes, I wanted a full meal,
and I knew the book that I would read, must read, though it felt
forbidden to an American girl raised on Jesus.
I mean the Koran. Curiosity became hunger,
as I needed to know what God it was I'd been fighting.
I wasn't alone. Many soldiers smelled the strange perfume
of Muslim culture, so alien yet so beautiful.

XIII.

"This time I learned about the man before I read the book.
I pledged myself not to judge from a Christian point of view,
and having been a soldier helped. Sometimes in this grim world,
we must kill or lose lives more dear, but a true soldier learns
to fight without hate and kill as the instrument of fate.
Muhammad's killing did not put his own emotions first,
and one can only know from battle the fierce part of God.

XIV.

"His use of sexuality was more bizarre to me;
for him it was another tool, to bind the loyalty
of tribal factions or exemplify a charity
he wanted to instill. Custom bends before a Prophet,
and strange as his practices seemed to me, I found nothing
bent but custom. So many worthy people trip on sex,
I wonder what constructing brace we need to walk upright.

XV.

"So I read the Koran and reread it, six months of work—
never before in my life was an effort so sustained.
It was shocking, confusing, calming, infuriating,
poignant, incomprehensible, visionary, simple,
wise, unequivocal, merciful, frightening and true.
In short, it provokes all reactions a person can have
to the presence of God and installs that presence to rule.

XVI.

"But in the end even as I could no longer follow
some Christian sect, I could not join Islam. Too weighted down
with culture, tradition, politics, the old religions
stifle the heart and busy the mind with changing the world.
In my heart, I am a Muslim, a Christian and a Jew,
and I would be a Buddhist too, had I studied enough
to find the Buddha in my heart, whose rhythm praises God.

XVII.

"Two things from the Koran I keep: the lesser principle
lights my reading and my effort to accept this brute world;
the greater guides every conscious moment of my being.
First, make no distinction among Prophets—the reminder
can come from Moses or Muhammad or the child next door.
Second, remembering Allah—being aware of God—
is a way of life, the state which measures meaning for us.

XVIII.

"After the Koran, I was different, and the healing
from Iraq was nearly done. I wanted an older story,
something great and ancient, venerable and enduring.
When I heard the oldest story, the epic of Gilgamesh,
was set in what is now Iraq, I thought that reading it
could be a chosen closing to the first half of my life.
I would attend this tale like the funeral of a friend.

XIX.

"What I found was both noble and shaggy, sympathetic
but also firm in its declaration of man's limit.
I did not read deep symbolism in it; the story
was enough for me then. So when I came to School and heard
it keyed around the steward, like *Hamlet* or the Gospels,
I sensed that there was something fundamental here, ancient
but now to be unearthed, to be discovered in my heart.

XX.

"You see, after I was called to School, this thing called steward
presented itself in great prominence; in our meetings
or in simple chats I heard the term. I asked about it
and was told it was the part in us, consolidating
over time, that wanted to work, that pressed in each moment
to make us more conscious. But I was too young in the work,
too scattered in my being, to hold this thing in myself.

XXI.

"I had also heard of the literary connections—
that Muhammad and Moses and Jesus were all stewards—
but didn't really understand that until we discussed
Marco's tale. Now I see how Odysseus and Gilgamesh
are also stewards. Prophets of God in the sacred texts
and heroes of culture in the great poems can be seen
as Heaven's tools, the best of mankind, awakening us."

XXII.

"Yes," said Carroll, "learning that key to understanding texts
changed everything for us. All that we hold essential now—
even our defining prayers—followed the epiphany
that Moses and Christ as well were stewards. Find the steward
in a sacred passage and the true meaning clarifies;
hear the steward in oneself and the work of the moment
becomes apparent. The steward's effort addresses God."

XXIII.

"But what does it mean," Ruby asked, "that the steward must die?"
"That part in us is not the soul, but the soul's great servant,"
Anamusa replied. "Thus the name steward. It recedes
when the soul emerges. Having done its work, it must die
symbolically, a sacrifice for the soul's presence.
And as presence is how we experience God, the soul
when fully present participates in God, is God."

XXIV.

"Yes, when I finished the book, I had an intuition,"
Ruby resumed, "a certainty without understanding
that Gilgamesh's failure was not mine, that what I was
was not flesh after all. This sense was not just a feeling—
a vague unfocused light—and of course I could not trust it,
but it proved the spool from which the thread of my life unwound.
I held that thread and searched past many veils to find you, friends."

XXV.

"You retraced your steps through the labyrinth," said Jules, his eyes
moist and open wide. "Yes," said Ruby. "At the time,
I had no sense of destination, but firmer footing
came as I realized I was ascending. I found you
in D.C. in a coffee shop. A bright conversation
overheard emboldened my approach, and I was welcomed."
"Every one of us has heard that story," said Jules, smiling.

XXVI.

"When was it truly born, this separation of my soul
from earth, this awareness? One cannot be aware of things
one is all in, but how and when does one begin to live
in the air, unsubmerged? It took the death of half my life
before my soul was strong enough to bear its own being,
to break the surface and breathe even a minute or two
before falling back under. Desperate the soul must be."

XXVII.

"Desperate to know itself, to return to God," said Jules.
"Return, return, return, always returning," said Mathilde.
"That's what the Koran says about David and Solomon,
if returning to God means repenting," Ruby affirmed.
"Returning to God is returning to presence," said Jules,
"and striving thus is the defining work of the steward."
"And there's no end," said Ana, "to our need of reminding."

XXVIII.

"That's what all the great stories are, all the sacred scriptures,
all the best epics," Carroll offered. "They are reminders,
large reminders full of small reminders urging return
to the present. But only for instructed men with eyes
to see and ears to hear. Most ride a tale just to enjoy
the ride. We note the reminders and our souls are summoned."
"Such sharing as this is the best reminder," Ruby said.

XXIX.

The morning was resplendent, and the airport terminal
had become a lighted prism. The cloudless sky promised
our patient gathering its long awaited home return.
Scattered travelers milled about; workers found their stations
and began the habits of day. Those still floating in sleep
would soon be washed ashore, delivered by the tide of light.
We stood and stretched and rubbed each other's shoulders lovingly.

XXX.

Marco and Mathilde departed down the hall, returning
soon with coffee, tea, sweet breads, jam and fruit. "For us," they beamed.
"At airport prices, you must have paid a fortune," Jules said.
"At friendship's prices, it was nearly nothing," they replied.
We took refreshment but did not forget our real purpose,
and after some moderate minutes our bright company
returned renewed attention to our Ruby. She began.

XXXI.

"Enkidu's death devastated the king. Death he had seen,
rude, abundant death, but the meaning of death had not seized
his heart before. Now death gripped Gilgamesh, fastened itself
to his throat and to the bottom of his spine and pushed him
back and down into the river of no breathing, no light.
So Gilgamesh writhed and struggled to return to the air,
and though his feet found the shore, he was drenched in death and dread.

XXXII.

"He and Enkidu had known the beginning and the end
of friendship, and the words that passed between them were golden
utterances of highest strain, the heartstrings' finest notes.
When Enkidu died, Gilgamesh waited weeks for the breath
of his friend to return. The truth of the corpse before him
suffused his understanding as water weakens a wall,
slowly, densely, until the stone dissolves within the flood.

XXXIII.

"To Ninsun his mother, prophetess and reader of dreams,
Gilgamesh went in distress. 'My friend, Enkidu, moves not,
and the slowest worms now devour him. O Mother, you know
many secrets and the designs of Heaven. Tell me now,
am I going to stop all movement and breath? Will I die
and become what Enkidu has become, an absent thing?
You've told me I am two-thirds God, yet I fear the death change.'

XXXIV.

"'You are as I've said, my son,' Ninsun replied, 'two parts God
and one part man, but the man the Gods have made has been made
to die, in their service if he is a great man, or lost
in the dreams of his mind, the net of his inheritance,
if he's a believer; but man is mortal nonetheless.'
'Mother, you bore me for this fate,' cried Gilgamesh. 'Why? Why?'
She replied, 'Serve Heaven. Your life cannot be more precious.'

XXXV.

"Gilgamesh stood up and proclaimed, 'I have heard flashes
of stories of a distant relative, Utnapishtim,
from whom the Gods removed their mortal curse, welcoming him
to their number. I will find him and by some means extract
from him the secret of not dying. Tell me how to start
my journey. You must give me the grace of that direction.
Have you no sorrow watching the death knot strangle your son?'

XXXVI.

"'A mother knows no greater woe than the death of her child,'
Ninsun whispered low, 'and I will know it. Stay with me, my son.
I can teach you the highest language of mortality.
You are King already. Be a hero for the ages.'
But in sudden knowledge of himself Gilgamesh replied,
'The dread effort of immortal knowledge must have my breath.
To stay would be to haunt myself with unaccomplished glory.'

XXXVII.

"Heavy with sorrow, Ninsun rose and with extended arm
directed his attention to the East. 'How far you'll walk,
what terrors face, I do not know, but you must find and cross
the Bitter Waters, one drop from which can poison your mind.'
With a resolve shocking to his mother, Gilgamesh spoke,
'However far I must go, I will find Utnapishtim
and wring from him the deathless knowledge. Mother, goodbye.'

XXXVIII.

"So began his search, the test of his will. In the desert
where it burned to stand, and the foul swamp where sucking worms found
all uncovered flesh, he kept his aim in his mind's forefront
and dismissed the whining thoughts that could not know the value
of his quest and so urged, begged and reasoned to forswear it.
Numb and meaningless had become the count of time, the past
and the future had dispersed before the great mountain appeared.

XXXIX.

"Like a high shelf above the world, there it was before him.
Its contours clarified as he approached, and then he saw
on a misty ridge a gathering of creatures, their fronts
all human but with great stinging scorpion tails rising
from behind. With their human arms they pointed straight at him,
and in an instant they were clicketing down the steep cliffs
as no mere men could move. He braced, and knew his fear as fear.

XL.

"Suddenly confronting him, their stark silence bade him speak.
'I am Gilgamesh, King of Uruk, a name and title
meaning nothing here. I seek Utnapishtim, who alone
among men does not die. I have vowed to find him and learn
from him the deathless secret. Will you help me or kill me?'
One whose human part was past midlife though still stalwart spoke,
'We are no threat, though what you seek to do has not been done.'

XLI.

"'Then I will be the first,' said Gilgamesh. 'Show me the way.'
The Scorpion leader sighed, 'Your stubbornness is granite,
like these mountains we defend, but what awaits you will melt
the most obdurate stone. I urge you, stay with us a month
and think past your quest. Within our limits, we men can do
noble deeds, but the Gods have placed deathlessness beyond us.'
'I ask only the way,' said Gilgamesh. 'The light is low.'

XLII.

"'There is no light at all where you are going. Your own hands
will be invisible to you. You'll not know where you step.
No food for your eyes or nose or ears, your thoughts will dissolve
into the puddle of fear you will become. Twelve dark leagues
you must pace, too far for a man. You will not remember
yourself or your breath, so lightless the serpentine caverns.
Why would you waste what the generous Gods have given you?'

XLIII.

"'Gilgamesh,' the Scorpion Man continued, 'my people
are stunning warriors who for aeons have defended
the sacred mountain, Mashu, from the low and unworthy.
We were told of your coming, that you were two parts divine,
one part man, and truly you are a wonder to observe.
But the man in you must learn his place in the Gods' grand scheme.
Even the best men, those who discourse with the sky, must die.'

XLIV.

"'Take me to the gate,' said Gilgamesh, 'unless you've been told
to deny me entrance. I must go on to the end
of the world or the end of my breath. That I will not see
is fitting, for I see no other meaning to my life.'
Said the other, 'It has been our task and honor to bar
the undeserving, but sorrowed am I now to let pass
such a noble one as you. Follow me down to the gate.'

XLV.

"At Mashu's base, disguised by overlapping walls of rock,
was a cleft opening down to darkness. There the small band
of Scorpion Men brought Gilgamesh. Their leader lifted
his arm to indicate the way, saying only, 'Behold.'
Turning his right foot toward the black hole, Gilgamesh thanked them
and marched into the bowels of earth with a firm resolve.
Before his second step touched ground, the darkness swallowed him.

XLVI.

"At first he moved through the thickening night with a clear head,
devising to count his steps, to give his mind a purchase
on the task. To break the twelve leagues into six divisions
was his plan, the number of steps in each league determined
by the simplest calculation of his strides. The sure trust
with which naïve straightforwardness measures what must be done
uplifted his spirits and drove him confidently on.

XLVII.

"At two leagues, as yet unbroken by his blindness, he'd charged
himself to hold pace, noting that he finished the first stage
but moving straight on. For several hundred steps, he felt
a slight descent and a corresponding cold coming on.
He was aware of his stride instinctively shortening
to meet the slope of the path, and the breathing underneath
his counting also shortened, and his count became unsure.

XLVIII.

"Soon he found himself wondering how far into that stage
he'd gone, and though his reckoning was accurate enough
to mark its end, he faced the third stage wavering, needy
of inspiration. He thought he heard ahead a whisper,
and his ears sharpened their attention, and sounds—were they there
or had he manufactured them?—came from all directions,
echoing and bleeding out in blended indistinction.

XLIX.

"Sensing the need of a single theme, an activity
of attention to keep his mind convergent and his pace
relentless, he chose this word as his constant conscious thought:
'Move!' And as he drove on through the still descending darkness,
that word in mind both pushed and pulled him forward, made single
all the tattered threads of thought that would unravel his aim.
Bottoming and frozen, he reached the end of the third stage.

L.

"Here and now, blind on the hard cold floor of the underworld,
Gilgamesh summoned himself to an effort greater still.
He turned and faced where he'd been but kept pace walking backwards,
and the path began to climb and turn, first this way, then that.
As the angle of ascent increased, his legs ached and burned,
but in that pain bearable as birth, he found his first sense
of certainty, and his heart held it as the earth a seed.

LI.

"Completing two leagues of steps and breaths, Gilgamesh returned
to forward and mounted the sinuous way, renewing
his earlier fixing thought—'Move!'—and his heart discovered
a new vigor, and though he continued to ascend and turn,
he found the going simpler, himself in control, and God
not withdrawn, a presence pulsing if unfathomable.
There! A glimmer of light and for an instant there was sight.

LII.

"With the final command, he firmed his mind and remembered
his training: 'Walk on, not to the end but past it, aware
of completion but trusting no thought of culmination.
Your task here finished, the next labor will make itself known.'
Thus confirmed, Gilgamesh left the blind underearth to meet
the full flood of light, and when the dazzle had subsided
into conscious seeing, he beheld the sacred garden.

LIII.

"In golden light enveloped there were palms and olive trees,
so orderly in arrangement and so fulfilled in form
that they seemed to understand how to please a higher sight.
And there were trees full of every kind of low hanging fruit,
plants and bushes flowering in colors unknown by words,
and to his ear the gentle bubbling of a nearby brook.
Here was abundance and beauty and the whisper of rest.

LIV.

"'But if all is perfect, what is this clenching within me?
I do not belong here.' Dropping his eyes to his body,
he saw the ripped rags that had become his clothes, the scratches
and scars covering his arms and legs. With the shriveled tips
of his fingers, he touched his face and found more broken skin
and a beard matted and wiry. 'I am a beggar here,
a blight on this place.' Suddenly his own name filled his ears.

LV.

"'Gilgamesh, we great Gods admire you in your role as King,
but no mortal has ever dared to touch his sandal down
in my sacred garden, and none ever will after you.
I, Shamash, God of the Sun, order you to leave this place
and all memory of it. Marvelous the human heart
that brought you here, but it is not welcome and you feel it.
Come back when your immortal parts are strong enough to rule.'

LVI.

"Said Gilgamesh, 'True, Shamash, I sense with tightening ribs
and throat my own alien presence here. I have found you
without meaning to. But what am I to do, fall to stink
and rot like Enkidu? It is unbearable to die,
to cease to be, and so I seek Utnapishtim, deathless
by the Gods' decree, and from him I will learn the secret.
Where will I find him? As you see, I will go anywhere.'

LVII.

"'Brave mortal,' said Shamash, 'follow the brook out of this place
down to the shore of the Sea of Time. A tavern keeper—
a woman, Siduri by name—will instruct you in all
a man may have and know. Forever here, death is your lot.'
From the clutch on his throat and the pain of breathing, the cold
in his groin and the icy emptiness claiming his mind,
the King knew he must obey and turned toward the brook's sweet sound.

LVIII.

"Walking beside the brook with laborious steps, he passed
out of the garden and at once felt a profound release.
The hand of death relaxed his clutch on his throat, breath returned,
and a flood of warmth surged through his trunk and out to his limbs.
Soon he was standing abundantly alive on the shore
of the Sea of Time, comfortable beside its great expanse,
wondering why a great man had no place in the garden.

LIX.

"Down the beach nine hundred steps, a small but sturdy structure
caught his eye. As he approached, the warm sand caressed
 his feet, and the gentle breeze swathed his skin with smooth delight.
At ease now, he walked straight to the front of Siduri's tavern,
put his foot across the threshold, only to feel the door
suddenly resist and slam against his presuming leg.
'Who are you, battered creature, who would come under my roof?'

LX.

"The voice was not full of fear, more indignance and offense.
The hero Gilgamesh, his strength and pride restored, replied in deep voice,
'I am Gilgamesh, Uruk's King, killer of Humbaba
and the great Bull of Heaven. I seek counsel, Siduri.'
'That you know my name means you've been sent,' said the wine seller,
'but you are scarred and unkempt, no dignity for my eye.
If truly Gilgamesh, know here you'll get nothing but truth.'

LXI.

"Sobering yet endearing were her words. 'No flattery
I seek,' he said. 'Too grave is my mission to indulge in lies.'
The door relaxed and resolutely in strode Gilgamesh,
certainty of purpose contradicting his ruined features.
One deep look into Siduri's eyes appeased his restlessness.
Here he would find the truth, as if from his mother, but more pure,
uncontaminated by the desire to protect him.

LXII.

"'Shamash will not have me in the garden,' said Gilgamesh,
and suddenly he felt himself dropping down to his knees
before her, unashamedly, his body submitting
but his mind in silent wonder. 'What's happening now?
Why do I crouch like a poor slave? Who are you, Siduri?'
'Better to ask who is Gilgamesh,' she replied calmly.
'The great hero Gilgamesh does not know his nothingness.'

LXIII.

"'I am King of Uruk whose walls are indomitable.
I mastered Humba--' 'Yes, yes I know,' she interrupted.
'I know all about your exploits. You have been disturbing
Heaven for a long time. Your twelve-leagues under earth
was worthy, and appearing in the garden to confront
Shamash was bold. No hero has ever done such a thing.
But the laws of the universe will not come down for you.'

LXIV.

"Baffled, Gilgamesh gazed back at her. At last he uttered,
'Then tell me who I am. Am I to die like Enkidu?'
'Gilgamesh must die,' said Siduri, giving no comfort,
'but what you truly are may live in the blessed garden
forever, serving an even greater God than Shamash.'
'I am hopelessly confused,' muttered the great Gilgamesh.
'I kneel helpless to the words of a woman of knowledge.'

LXV.

"Siduri laughed, 'Gilgamesh is a machine, invented
to be mastered, that what you truly are can separate.
As long as you are he, your fate is to be discarded
like a tool no longer needed. You are stuck in the role
of Gilgamesh, the one-third mortal part of you, the shell,
the earthly shape. You do not know yourself. God has not yet
visited you. You are an unannihilated lie.'

LXVI.

"'I have no reply to this,' said Gilgamesh. 'What you say
fits nowhere in my understanding. I am as I've been.'
'Exactly. You are the body unaware of the soul.
You believe the world and would do great things to leave your mark.
You are noble, Gilgamesh, and your courage shocks the Gods;
you are a builder of cities, an artist, a hero,
but what is a hero but desire in a mold of dust?'

LXVII.

"'Then what can a man do?' he cried. 'Can a man do nothing?'
'Men move things around,' she replied. 'Dirt, sticks and stones, altars,
temples, cities, empires, words, ideas, values, beliefs.
Around man goes, pushing things and thoughts in his cage of time.
Man must know his nothingness to return to God, to merge—
though adding nothing in the merger—and become again
what he's always been. Man dies but can die before he dies.'

LXVIII.

"'I am at a loss,' sighed Gilgamesh. 'Should I kill myself?'
'Not yourself, but Gilgamesh. The Gilgamesh lie must die.'
From his bowels he felt a surging strength, and suddenly
he was standing, erect, bristling, his whole head above hers.
'Enough of these womanly mysteries,' he roared at her.
'Tell me where to find Utnapishtim. From a deathless man
I'll claim the deathless spell. Point the way, Siduri. No tricks.'

LXIX.

"She faced him without fear or awe. 'You have been instructed,
but barely,' she said. 'It will take a hard situation
to elicit what I've given you and make you use it.
Were you patient, I could round and smooth the teaching to fit
your very breathing, but you are a man as unaware
as you are strong and restless. Urshanabi minds his boat
a league down shore. You'll need him to cross the Bitter Waters.'

LXX.
"'And I will cross them,' boasted Gilgamesh. 'Though I know not
for what, I thank you.' He strode out the tavern door intense
and purposeful, moving on to the next link in the chain.
He covered the league as a fire devours grassland, finding
the ferryman's boat unattended. Gilgamesh screamed
with enflaming ire, 'Urshanabi, boatman, show yourself.
You have a passenger, I, Gilgamesh, King of Uruk.'

LXXI.

"But no answer came, and in Gilgamesh began to burn
a great wrath. 'Urshanabi!' he bellowed to break the sky,
but still no reply, no presence coming forth to greet him.
In a maddened rage, Gilgamesh ripped and smashed what his hands
could grasp, tearing from the boat its nets and cables, slashing
its furled sail, his internal storm breaking cracks in the mast.
Then a voice: 'You're a man wrestling with himself in the grave.'

LXXII.

"Panting and exhausted, Gilgamesh let drop from his hands
the shreds of the tackle he had savaged. In heaving voice
still riding on the crashing waves of his breath, he thundered,
'You must know my name. You will take me to Utnapishtim.'
Urshanabi waited to speak, checking his own anger.
'I can take you nowhere, you self-destroying animal.
What you have ruined keeps me safe sailing the Bitter Waters.'

LXXIII.

"'Then I'll go in your boat alone without a mast or sail.'
'Go if you must,' Urshanabi replied, 'but the currents
will have their way with you and determine your landing place.
These simple tools that you have disrespected are the friends
of sailors for all time. They are proof against accident
and let us plan our destination. Man's luck is not so good
that he can find the other shore by trusting the water.'

LXXIV.

"'I am going on,' said Gilgamesh, 'even without hope.'
And the heart of Urshanabi stirred in admiration
of the reckless King, and he loved him as he would a son.
'There is one other way to navigate,' the boatman said.
'It is primitive and tedious work and allows us
only shallow water progress. We can stay near the shore
and move by poling, thrusting forward again and again.'

LXXV.

"'Whatever must be done, I will do it. I will go now
into the forest and cut poles. How many will we need
and of what size? Tell me, Urshanabi. Be clear and quick.'
'The boat will hold one hundred twenty; we will need them all,
probably more,' the boatman answered. 'Each pole must measure
sixty cubits in length, and you must coat them with a thick pitch
and reinforcing ferrules that allow your hands a grip.'

LXXVI.

"Before Urshanabi finished, Gilgamesh was moving
toward the forest. There he worked tirelessly for many days
preparing the poles, pitching and ferruling them, dragging
them back to the boat and stacking them high. His mighty axe
made a rough, discordant music that disturbed the kind Gods,
who by now had grown tolerant of the desperate quest
of Gilgamesh. 'Such a noisy creature is man,' some thought.

LXXVII.

"With the poles stacked on deck, the boat sat low in the water,
and Urshanabi groaned that the journey was too risky.
Gilgamesh dismissed the old man's fear, urging him to stay.
'Just give me direction. I'll go alone. Do not hazard
your life for my aim,' said Gilgamesh without taunting.
But Urshanabi waded out and climbed aboard with care,
and Gilgamesh gave a great push then swung his legs on deck.

LXXVIII.

"The current carried them slowly toward the Bitter Waters,
and for three days neither spoke. More turbid and noisome grew
the water as they went, till at last a foul stench rose
to enwrap them as would a cloud. Coughing hard, the boatman
pointed to the poles and said, 'Now.' Gilgamesh seized the first
and thrust it into the water till he felt it bottom.
The boat lurched forward, but the pole dissolved in the King's hand.

LXXIX.

"'Do not let your hands touch the water,' Urshanabi warned.
With pole after pole did Gilgamesh drive the boat forward
only to have them disappear in his hands, eaten up
by the all-dissolving Bitters Waters. With but ten poles
remaining, the other shore came vaporously in sight.
'There!' cried Gilgamesh, his heart exulting as he pointed.
But soon the last pole had gone, and the shore seemed no closer.

LXXX.

"'We've had no luck with the current,' Urshanabi sorrowed.
Exhausted, breathing like a great bellows, Gilgamesh dropped
to one knee in mournful dejection. 'I am a dead man,
a rotting thing drying up in other men's memories.'
'You destroyed the gear and sail, Gilgamesh,' said Urshanabi,
and all your ruthless audacity fell to accident.
Now we must wait to see where the Bitter Waters leave us.'

LXXXI.

"Gilgamesh stood in the center of the boat, unfastened
his garment and clutching its folds bared his heart to Heaven.
He raised his eyes and extended his arms in humble prayer.
'Shamash and the rest of you, Gods who rule the earth and men,
I challenge you no more. You are all, and I am nothing.
I ask for no mercy or favor, only let me be
what I am to be in the great order you have made.'

LXXXII.

"Instantly the little boat shuddered in the foul water
and began to urge forward, gathering speed and moving
toward the foggy shore. Still fixed in prayer, Gilgamesh
became aware of himself as one with the gliding boat.
'Be still,' said Urshanabi. 'You have made yourself the mast,
and your spread garment is acting as our sail. Do not move.
No thoughts or sentiments now. Give yourself to the Gods' wind.'

LXXXIII.

"And so Gilgamesh stood, arms extended, a man become
a mast, aware but insensate in his resolution,
while his garment billowed lightly in the foul, fetid air.
Effortlessly flowed his breath, his chest rising and falling
in atunement to a greater rhythm, acting its duty
in perfect obedience, while his eyes rose to Heaven,
relaxed in their sockets, and shining tears streamed down his face.'

LXXXIV.

"From his wedded head and heart insight came, 'So wrong I've been.'
And he knew the truth of his thrust for immortality—
all vanity and fear, all service to the wrong master—
and he longed for the disburdening death of Gilgamesh,
the fleshy thing, the personality, the character
of muscle and rage, for he knew that which he truly was
died not, and he slipped from the noose of his imagined self.

LXXXV.

"And the free thing that he was rose skyward and looked back down
on the human frame fixed in its purpose, and the two parts
knew themselves now, male and female, joined in airy congress,
one being: a mystic marriage of higher elements.
This soul out of time knew kinship with all who know the truth,
and in the flash of an eternal instant all that was
was taken into God and therein dissolved in union.

LXXXVI.

"When he identified himself again, having drifted
back down the ray of being, he knew that to his poor flesh
he must return, to forget and remember this transport
again and again, a memory become a longing,
until the death of Gilgamesh restored eternity
unbroken; thus he accepted the folly of this life
with the fixed certainty of him who guards the Pyramids.

LXXXVII.

"And then he again was Gilgamesh, still eager but wise,
still in the posture of supplication, disciplined prayer,
holding, holding, holding his being and thus shouldering
a share of God's suffering. Still full of bright love, his eyes
met those of Urshanabi, and the two, now wordless friends,
watched as the brave little boat glided toward the other shore
and the echoing joke of Utnapishtim's deathlessness."

LXXXVIII.

Ruby ceased and patiently let go a long stream of breath.
"That was marvelous," said Marco. "I'm sure I'm not alone
in my surprise at your knowledge and bold authority.
You were a child to us; now also you are a steward
in the work who came to us mature in will. We thank you."
"I'm gratified by what you say, Marco, but no credit
can I take for the tale. I was but the sail in its breeze."

LXXXIX.

"Exactly," said Jules. "That is all we are. The rest is done
by the Gods and the spirits they direct. We are their tools."
"Telling the story," said Ruby, "was as you said before—
my mind was running to catch up to the words issuing
from my mouth. I spoke the story but was not the teller."
"Look at what goes on around us now," said Mathilde. "We sail
on a sea with men who are unaware of the water."

XC.

The airport had returned to full activity. The drone
quickly filled our ears as the valves of our focus relaxed.
"I'll see where we stand," said Marco. He rose serenely
and walked toward the counter, a queue already there to join.
"We've waited so long," said Mathilde, "but I want the last tale.
"We are this work now," said Ana, "and want only the time
to finish this great prayer we've started before we're called home."

End, Book Five

Book Six: *An Egyptian Life*

I.

Waiting for Marco's return, Carroll spoke. "Competing thoughts
about the final story wrestle in my mind. To fit
the form we have grown into, it must be the longest one
if only by a small measure. And as you remember
from our earlier talk, we wanted an Egyptian tale,
one that pays tribute to the source of esoteric work.
I have two candidates, but I need your advice to choose."

II.

Jules' reply was almost an interruption, startling us
with its quickness. "My dear Carroll, you must not feel constrained
to praise Egypt as our tradition's origin. Our work
is as old as man, or as the Gods' interest in man.
We have evidence from thousands of years before Egypt."
"True, Jules," Carroll agreed, "but Egypt offers us the first
mature and complete expression of it, worthy of praise."

III.

"What did you mean by 'two candidates'?" Ana wondered.
"And on what basis are we to choose?" asked Mathilde softly.
"If they're both Egyptian stories, perhaps we need to know
their chief difference," Ruby offered. Carroll seemed amused.
"It's clear by the speed of the conversation that a night
without sleep has not weakened us. I needn't fear your lapse
of attention," he said, "nor can I hide a poor effort."

IV.

He continued, "The mythology of Egypt presents us
with many remarkable tales bizarre and quickening
to our minds. Because of our studies, such tales elicit
our efforts and reinforce our grip on the here and now.
From that fund of wonder, I can offer my favorite,
the story of Osiris and Isis, or some others
if your prefer, but something beckons from another realm."

V.

"How do you mean?" asked Mathilde. As if uncomfortable
in his chair, Carroll shifted and crossed his legs and looked down.
"O my, this gets interesting," mused Ana. "You might as well
run through the whole repertoire of the gestures of unease—
clear your throat, pull your earlobe, scratch your beard. Dear Carroll,
what can be the root of this reticence? What's so shocking
it can turn joviality to boyish bashfulness?"

VI.

"Yes, Carroll," asked Jules, growing very curious, " please tell us
what the other story is that can so fluster our friend.
Is it a steamy tale of sexual intrigue and crime?"
"Or perhaps an unsophisticated rustic fable
that embarrasses your eloquence," suggested Ana.
Carroll sat straight up and gathered himself. "My friends, I'm sure
you could not guess the type of my tale were we here a year."

VII.

"But it must touch Egypt, must it not?" asked Ruby. "That promise
still holds, I hope." Carroll smiled at her benevolently
and reassured her. "I have not abandoned Egypt, dear."
"Let us give him the space to explain," asserted Mathilde.
"Yes, though I've overheard only the last few words, I'm caught
in this web," said Marco, rejoining us and taking part.
"Ah, but first what news?" asked Carroll. "What of our going home?"

VIII.

"They have told me we will be called individually.
We have no way of knowing in what order, but no one
going where we're going can expect to leave before noon."
Quickly digesting Marco's information, we discerned
there was nothing to be done but to be just where we were
listening to Carroll's story. "We are free to finish
our game!" Ruby proclaimed, and that clarity made us glad.

IX.

"Now, Carroll," said Ana, "tell us more about this strange tale
so unsettling you seek the group's permission to tell it.
Carroll took a deep breath and exhaled, and the smallest smile
formed on his lips and floated there like the simplest of boats
on the kindest river. "I will tell you all that I know—
how the story came to me, how it has affected me—
then you can decide if it should be told or held private."

X.

Already we were struggling to govern our attention,
not to fall head first into this delicious mystery.
"I was twenty-four," he began, "years before Heaven called,
and my little life was falling apart. I had a job
proofreading for a magazine, but it paid so little
and my stylish wife looked so longingly on so many things
she wanted, I could tell the marriage had not long to last.

XI.

"Being uninstructed, I thought I had to trust my thought,
which fumed in conflict and travail and offered no way out.
To my sight today, the whole dread circumstance seems childish,
but then it felt like being crushed breathless between boulders.
I sought a counselor, a psychiatrist. As I dressed
on the day of my appointment, my young wife was packing.
I brought the doctor a state of helplessness and turmoil.

XII.

"She led me through the usual preliminary course,
her questions unabrasive, her tone of studied kindness,
but halfway through the short hour, as she plumbed my history,
our conversation took an abrupt and shocking detour.
When she asked if I'd ever known my current state before,
I came quite out of myself, and from my mouth there issued
a flow of utterance, more like a sybil's mystic chant."

XIII.

"Pictures formed in the center of my forehead, episodes
as if on a screen, and I found myself narrating them.
Effortlessly the pictures became a spoken story
which I listened to my voice deliver, and all the while
I realized that I was watching myself, not the man
whose form you know, but the true self I am, its history
in another body, a distant life lived long ago."

XIV.

"What did the doctor do with this bizarre issue?" asked Jules,
betraying no disturbance on his face or in his tone.
"I think she thought I was having a psychotic seizure
of some kind," Carroll said, "but I was not out of control
or vehement or troubled." "All the more eerie," said Jules.
"You're right. It must have been shocking. She wanted to prescribe
some strong medication, but I left and did not return."

XV.

"And that was the end of it? asked Ana, a slight quaver
in her voice. "I would think she would have pursued the matter."
"She may have called. I had no answering machine back then.
A bill did come, and with the check I sent a polite note
thanking her and indicating that I felt much better."
"When gaps in the curtain of reality fly open,
it can be terrifying," said Jules in a soothing tone.

XVI.

"And what did you make of this experience?" asked Ana.
"I simply recorded it," said Carroll. "Other trouble
kept me from investigating. My wife filed for divorce.
The bills piled up. I had to find a better paying job.
There was barely room for sorrow, much less for real research."
"Did the episode remain vivid in mind?" asked Marco.
"Yes," said Carroll. "That was my proof of its integrity."

XVII.

 "And the story you discovered then is the same story
you would tell us now?" asked Mathilde in audible alarm.
"If you'll hear it. It touches Egypt in a way fitting
our discovered purpose. Of course, if anyone objects,
being too skeptical or finding this matter queasy,
I'll defer to your judgment and tell a less troubling tale.
"What a remarkable opportunity!" Marco chimed.

XVIII.

"How do you mean?" asked Ana, who had moved intimately
close to Mathilde and seemed to be speaking for both of them.
"We have a chance to assess a story unknown to us
on its own merits," Marco replied. "I'm sure we all trust
Carroll's heart never to intentionally deceive us,
so we'll be able to focus purely on the story."
The ladies kept their firm silence, their blessing yet withheld.

XIX.

With Mathilde clutching her hand, Anamusa spoke at last,
measuring her syllables, intoning them precisely.
"You know, Carroll, I have no doubt of your integrity.
I am sure you will give us the story as it happened
in the doctor's office and as you have since preserved it,
but as you've introduced it, your story itself asserts
a troublingly subjective claim to a past life of yours."

XX.

"That is my theory of what it is," assented Carroll.
"What else might it be?" asked Ruby forthrightly. "For myself,
I could not distinguish between a past life episode
and a tale heard in early childhood at my grandma's knee."
"There is nothing in our teaching about the influence
of previous lives," said Mathilde, a worry in her voice.
"So quickly could this kind of thing erode into a séance."

XXI.

"But the teaching does make allowance for previous lives.
That multiple lifetimes are needed for awakening
has been with us since early on," Marco reminded us.
Mathilde held firm. "That idea is as much metaphor
as doctrine, a way of designating level of work.
The Teacher has not given systematic instruction
in this area. We are lying if we believe it."

XXII.

"That much is certainly true," said Jules. "Believing the world
defiles eternity, whether we fix on Carroll's tale
or some small run of our own trouble. Surely we know this.
We are schooled not to fall into belief – or disbelief."
"But this is the last entry in our game," declared Ana,
"a game that has become much more. I, for one, do not want
a dilution or anticlimax. It would offend art."

XXIII.

At this the men could not restrain their mirth. Their smiles spread wide.
"So smudging the teaching is not your real concern," said Jules.
"Of course it is," protested Ana. But as you say, Jules,
I can protect my internal work. But what we've made here
deserves a noble ending, not an accidental close."
"Ana," said Jules earnestly, "each who has told a story
has noted the sense of a higher mind directing it."

XXIV.

"Lest there be any contention, I will withdraw the tale.
I can offer other possibilities," said Carroll.
"Wait, Carroll," Marco urged. "The tale from the dark of your mind
may or may not be a past life story, but you must think
it a suitable culmination of our construction.
I trust you, Carroll. You would not sacrifice our efforts
to triviality or vanity. I know your heart."

XXV.

With this, a wise silence ensued, the silence of people
who know the limits of words and argument. I listened
to my own internal prayers which proceeded without harm.
Suddenly trickling down from my forehead came a thought known
and cherished. "The solution is always at a level
higher than the problem." Had I spoken? All the eyes turned
to me as if awaiting oracular utterance.

XXVI.

"Go a head, William," said Mathilde, smiling. "We have heard
so little from you. Perhaps you should tell our last story."
"Mathilde, the very thought of that makes me wobble and faint.
I am no story teller. I simply record the art
that others more practiced than I have offered to please us."
Mathilde pressed on. "Are you troubled by concluding our round
with a tale so dangerously subjective and unknown?"

XXVII.

I tried to speak with respect, gentleness and discretion.
"Mathilde, you began our round with a simple intention,
which you fleshed out with your experience and good humor;
but let us remember that your tale ended with a dream,
whether an actual dream or a narrative conceit
I do not know. Either way, it was a perfect closing,
unexpected, shuddering us back to seriousness."

XXVIII.

With a small bow of her head, Mathilde acknowledged this truth.
"If it matters," she said, "it was a real dream. I am not
that skilled at invention and must rely on what the Gods
put in my head. I believe I see your point, William."
"So do I," said Marco. "As Buddha ate whatever food
was dropped into his bowl, so we tell whatever stories
the Gods put in our heads, but we think ourselves the craftsmen."

XXIX.

"We are reciters who believe ourselves to be authors."
"So it seems, Jules," I continued. Is it not so that all
who have told tales have acknowledged that the tales told themselves,
that they were but mouths for stories coming forth from a mind
and will beyond? If we can trust that Heaven has control,
then the story—whatever we believe to be its source—
will be delivered as the Gods intend—form and content."

XXX.

"It is a lovely attitude," said Ana, "as befits
a devoted young man, but where do I tie my camel?"
"So you are afraid of our capacity to distort
a true message?" asked Ruby. How is that not a belief?'
"I would say"—and here I chose my words as a chef chooses
peaches for his king's desert—"the bowl of experiment
is on the table. We're not rebels or innovators."

XXXI.

Another silence followed, and slowly like a fair scent
a general satisfaction settled over the friends.
Finally Ana spoke with resolution, "If silence
is the form of our agreement, then let the tale be told."
"May we retain the right," asked Mathilde in earnest, "to stop
the flow of narrative for questions? Not interruptions
but sincere inquiry. I need reins to ride this strange horse."

XXXII.

"Bright questions are most needed in this matter," said Carroll.
"I've been carrying this text around for years, unable
to translate it fully. I hope the opportunity
to put it before you now is neither an accident
nor a vanity. That it is an Egyptian story
gives me hope that this venue is its right destination.
Sincere and forthright questions can only help unveil it."

XXXIII.

With that Mathilde completely relented. "Carroll," she said,
"you know I love you, and my respect for you is profound.
Do not let my skittishness summon up in you the pall
of custom. When we are not present—here and now—learned forms
control and regulate our values. It is true the world
can't survive without such dominance, but my calling on
that force to subjugate an instructed man wrongs two souls."

XXXIV.

"Thank you, Mathilde," responded Carroll. "Now I can begin.
First let me say that what you will receive is a series
of sharp scenes around which I will speculate a story.
The scenes are exactly as they came to me, a sequence
vivid and definitive. They have a self-evident
progress and need no narrative connection, but there's good
in distinguishing these episodes from my deductions.

XXXV.

"The first scene takes place in a primitive land above Kush,
that is, south of Nubia. The scenes to follow move north
through regions watered by the Nile, arriving in Egypt,
so I locate the first scene south of more civilized
territory, among hunter-gatherers, in grasslands
semi-arid but not inhospitable to humans
who demand little from the earth to make their livelihood.

XXXVI.

"The time, again concluded from subsequent scenes, can be
set about three thousand five hundred years ago, in what
has been labeled Egypt's Second Intermediary,
between the Middle and New Kingdoms, though the trappings
of an advanced civilization have little to do
with our beginning. The first is the simplest, a single
impression of determining power in a young life.

XXXVII.

"A watering hole, an emergent spring whose few dozen
liters a day feed the trees that shadow it and sustain
a varied wildlife: there a dark man camouflaged by shade
has raised a specialized spear, but one of many carried
for him by a boy behind. I am that boy; the man
is my father, poised to make a killing throw; a gazelle
twenty meters on drinks its last, unmindful of its death.

XXXVIII.

"How poised and patient is my father! Actively he waits
until the moment opens to a perfect angle made
by the neck of the prey stretched just a little awkwardly
so that it cannot bolt and run in one lightening movement.
The caste, a silent seamless arc of mind and shoulder, sends
the death point over the planned distance with merciful speed.
The creature jerks, crumbles at the knees, lists and loses breath.

XXXIX.

"Again my father's aim brings home a feast for many.
He is the master, I his apprentice in this great work,
but I am troubled in the heart and absorb his knowledge
like a staining fluid, corrupting me within, clogging
the portals of gladness—for my father, for my people.
What am I to do with this burden of disgust? The tribe
looks to me to be my father's arm carried on through time.

XL.

"We are known as the people of the spear. Our great knowledge
of that weapon sets us apart, gives us stability,
as no people can survive without a special knowledge
that makes necessity submit to the desire for life.
On the walls in the houses of our men are hung hundreds
of hunting spearpoints each for a singular animal
and circumstance, and thirty shafts matched by weight to the prey.

XLI.

"Having trained a generation of our men to hunt,
even as his father trained him, my father now trains me,
the son he waited so long for, the flesh of his own flesh.
But I am not my father, not his flesh, not flesh at all.
I am an exile here in this land among these people
in this body nearing manhood. Of these I claim nothing.
I breathe only as a fumbling blunt assertion: I am.

XLII.

"Why can I not accept my father's world? Why do I hold
my breath when he instructs me? The men of our tribe are good,
sincere, familial; it is true their hearts walk not
their own course but ride on their stomachs, but of what people
can this not be said? They are not to blame, and my father,
best among them, deserves a better scion. His quiver
of spear shafts, an honor to carry, abuses my neck.

XLIII.

"As if born already finished with this hunter's knowledge,
venerable but cold ash to my heart, I long to leave,
though I have no destination, no hope of greater truth.
There is no arguing with my father, no discussion
with children. He cannot hear the echoes of emptiness.
From perhaps a dozen moments treasured in memory,
I love him, but far more do I feel bleak admiration.

XLIV.

"Perhaps I wait to the hunting phase of the manhood rite—
three days alone when no one would track me. Taking no rest
I travel, not in haste but in quickened resolution,
east to the river, the great boundary, the definer
of earth life. Dare I cross? I doubt it, but follow it
north, toward the storied realm of city dwellers shiny black.
Split from the past, knowing nothing, a walking man I am."

XLV.

Carroll paused. "Ah, now I am intrigued," said Jules, "and I hope
you forgive our skeptical shiverings. The tale wins out."
"I must agree," Anamusa offered. "This fine morsel
you've served us already reveals esoteric content."
"And have you warmed to the tale, my dear?" Marco asked Mathilde.
"I'm withholding judgment," she replied, "but I'm not averse
to hearing more. The scene you painted was truly poignant."

XLVI.

"I would take credit for some artistry," Carroll returned,
"but the scenes were given to me entirely as they are,
and so I offer them. The narration here and there now
bears the freight of my research, but I've changed nothing. I've tried
to discover what facts are studded in these scenes and let
those facts give anchor to this 'unpremeditated art.'
There's Milton's phrase again; perhaps he is observing us."

XLVII.

"Does our young man have a name?" Ruby asked. Silence followed
as we preserved the marvel of her practicality.
"I'm afraid not," admitted Carroll. "The story comes forth
in first person narrative, no name revealed. Would you have us name him?
'Let's be careful,' said Marco. "Sentimentality lurks."
"If you promise that confusion won't arise, then no name
is needed," said Ruby, "but let's get on to the next scene."

XLVIII.

Carroll smiled with quiet affection. "As you wish," he said.
"For many days I walk beside the river, finding shade,
frequently refreshing myself at it banks. More than once
I'm beckoned by boatmen moving up and down, but I wave
and refuse hospitality, fearing captivity.
The dried food in my sack, which I'd thought abundant, dwindles;
I'm left to eat the small fish I can snare at wading depth.

XLIX.

"At night I am frightened of sleeping, and I make no fires,
do nothing to attract thieves or slavers; up in the trees
I climb where braced by thick branches and hidden by foliage
I nap an hour or two at a time. But I encounter
no real threat, and the glaring days of northbound walking
see hunger grow and fear subside. The blisters on my feet
trouble me more than scavengers, human or animal.

L.

"Finally one morning, the sun halfway to its zenith,
I realize the dirty haze clinging between the ground
and the sky far off is a sign of men, not nature's work.
Is this the mark of a city? I walk on all that day
and half another, the foul air denser, more palpable
as I approach. I seek a height, a rocky outcropping,
and climb. By the time I reach the top my feet are bleeding.

LI.

"Stretched before me is a vast settlement of mud and smoke,
beside the river, as if left behind by a great flood
retreating back into its banks. Instinctively, a cough
and a gagging spasm arise from me as my body
struggles to cleanse itself of what my eyes are taking in.
Yet though the sight disgusts me, I know as I knew to leave
my tribe that I am venturing there. I hope not to stay."

LII.

Again Carroll paused, but this time no one spoke, allowing
him to gather himself to continue. "From what I've learned,
this was most likely Kerma, the Nubian capital.
I have no sense of what followed there, chaotic fragments
only—a bazaar full of cackles and strange aromas,
lines of archers black as night arrayed before a palace.
The dominant impression even now is one of fear.

LIII.

"In the next true scene I have, the boy walks behind a man,
by his skin not a Nubian. The boy's feet are healing,
salved and bandaged by an expert hand, and behind them creep
a train of three donkeys, carrying a great weight of goods
bartered for in Kerma. We head north northeast following
the river. Days and days we travel before the first town
appears; at night he teaches me words, shards of his language.

LIV.

"Finally we arrive at a great fort, a citadel
from which one can scan the river and the desert around it.
My master is visibly relieved, and greets the soldiers
in his language. There are Nubian archers also there,
but those like my master are in charge. By one we are called,
led to a room where lies a soldier with a deadly wound.
Bowing gratefully, those around the bed make room for us.

LV.

"Now I understand my master is a healer, known here
and respected. The soldier has been stabbed in his right side;
the blood still oozes, more black than red. My master orders
me to bring a package from our stores. With a poultice made
from herbs and flour, he packs the wound, instructing his patient
in a breathing exercise. The soldier still lives next day
when we leave this safe place with a caravan headed north.

LVI.

"Around the night fires I learn whom I am traveling with—
'Asians-in-Egypt' they call themselves. While they address
my master as a friend, it is clear he's not one of them.
I have not the skill to speak, to ask where we are going.
Knowing nothing, I am my own destination, holding
myself to the simplest perceptions, glad simply to be.
The desert is all we see for days, but I am not dismayed.

LVII.

"We are up before dawn, traveling all morning. Near noon
we look for vegetation, the smallest indication
of water. There we dig a shallow well, stop for the day
and wait for evening. Then we travel on till sunset.
Forty days of this. Then one morning, two hours after dawn,
the desert goes green, and greener as we move. Oasis!
A vast garden breathes, resting on a river underground.

LVIII.

"I do not know it yet, but I am home. The caravan
replenishes its stores of wood and water and moves north.
My master leads me, two more days of fertile farms and palms.
We arrive at a village where all the inhabitants,
as if signaled by Heaven, wait for us, fruit and flowers
in their outstretched hands, true gladness beaming from their faces.
Amazed, I wonder what my work will be in Paradise."

LIX.

Carroll's breathing slowed and found an even rhythm. No sound
came forth from any of us; we wanted more of the tale,
but we saw that he could only bring it forth in chapters,
laboring to hold the state in which the images rose
and poured their words. Silently summoning patience, we held
attention for him, not letting this crystal moment crack.
The slightest smile appeared on Carroll's face as he resumed.

LX.

"Fifteen years I spend there, doubling my age, learning the art
of healing from my master. In earthly terms, this period
is the happiest of my life, though it's not yet the true
flowering of purpose. At eighteen, I receive as wife
my master's daughter; two years on, my own daughter is born.
At twenty-four, I assume my master's daily work
when he ventures to Kerma to trade for the next year's stores.

LXI.

"His art is based on judgment more than knowledge or technique,
a sense of when to act and when to wait. A physician
cannot defy nature; he is a handmaid to healing,
restoring straightness in the bone and balance in the breath.
Often it is enough to relieve pain and let a soul
make peace with the source to which it must return. Do not think,
ye craftsmen, that the skilled blade performs the true work. Know God.

LXII.

"The best and worst of duties is childbirth. When nature sets
 herself to the task, all the pain and toil have fruition:
a soul has form to strive against and grow strong mastering.
But when nature sours, resists with her shoulders the portal's
opening, and life is bludgeoned in the passage, the tears
of the mother and the helpless sighs of the healer bring
nothing home. Then bitter sorrow must be transformed. Know God.

LXIII.

"Attending the tearing points in the soul's earthly garment,
the healer rides on poignancy but keeps his seat upright.
He works amid pain and fear, labor and expectation,
hope and guilt, courage and despair. He will be drawn in, seized
and dragged down into the blood and believing, but he must
free himself, clean to purity the vessel of his heart,
give his hands to the meaning in suffering and know God.

LXIV.

"There in the oasis, I learn the range and boundaries
of humanity. Whole hearted and glad, I greet the sun
and am a friend among friends. I am not proud of my place
but grateful, and though I obey an outward God, I seek
no more than what I have, what man can have of earth's bounty.
Thus I am not ready for the inward God, the real God,
when all turns suddenly dire and what I know is waste.

LXV.

"For knowing God is a higher, harder birth, more in truth
a rebirth, out of the womb of earthlife, its smothering
embrace. From all that earth encloses—the identity
we weave from her ready strands—we must separate and find
ourselves distinct, a consciousness apart, liberated
in the pain of parturition. Only then can we know God.
I am not ready when my first chance comes to be reborn.

LXVI.

"Troubled by my master's puzzlement, I watch as he pores
over the purple swollen throats and chests of a young couple.
Many in their quarter are ill, they say, but assume time
will do the healing. He escorts them back to their dwelling
and wraps their throats and heads in a treated bandage, gives them
herbs to make a potent, wretched tea. In two days they die,
and my master has discolored lips and a choking cough.

LXVII.

"The deaths begin in earnest—dozens in that dread quarter
lie down and depart. My master declines and has no art
to check this disease and its spread. He falls in front of me
as we drag a sled of bodies to the sands far outside town.
'Burn the bodies,' he tells me, and then he is one of them.
For three days I am destruction, making devouring fire;
no one will look at me or help with this unholy work.

LXVIII.

"Going home, exhausted, I trudge down streets devoid of life.
The dead lie outside each house, the waiting-to-die within.
This plague so fast and silent, no thought of escape could form.
Why am I not among them? I have no symptoms, no pain.
I watch the throes of my town as if from a vulture's perch
on the crown of my own head. I arrive to find my wife
and daughter huddled in disease. They die in my embrace.

LXIX.

"In less then a week, I alone, the adopted one, move
in a ruin of corpses. In shock at God's sudden madness,
leveled by my own survival, I gather what I can
of food, water, money, and walk north toward our neighbor town,
but far outside of it, I am menaced by a patrol
of armed men firing arrows in warning to stay away.
To them I am a disease; I turn right, east, toward the river.

LXX.

"I go on, why or how long I do not know. If I live,
the river awaits at some point, under the rising sun.
After some days, the habits of desert travel revive
in me—resting the blank days uncaring, pacing the nights.
Total loss is liberation if the heart does not turn
to stone, but how can it not? The feet walk on—that is all.
I smell the river and the city before I see them.

LXXI.

"Distinct in my nose are two fumes: one foul and burnt, calling
back the visceral disgust of my dead town; the other
cool and humid, underneath the first, breathing a promise.
I seek a height and know from doing so I am not dead.
The climbing sun illuminates a city, another
to the north, another farther on. The river binds them
like a stitching thread. What's left of my life is to be here."

LXXII.

Again Carroll paused and his eyes dropped. The morning hubbub
rushed into our ears, and the light of our own climbing sun
poured in, a warming illumination and reminder
of the permanent aim to which we were all devoted.
I surprised myself by enquiring, "Do you need a break?"
"Just a few breaths," Carroll replied. "Let me not lose this strange
remembered life until its purpose shines in clarity."

LXXIII.

He resumed and his first syllable firmed our attention.
"My grief gives way to fear, inordinate fear, as I move
through the sparse settlement on the west bank of the river.
I have no knowledge, no language which can secure me here.
Everyone I pass seems to pause in their movements and look
at me, a bereft stranger. My eyes sink down to avoid
the eyes of others. I steer a course through shadows of men.

LXXIV.

"In the next glimpse, I am once again following a man.
We arrive at river's edge and board a broad-sailed boat
with a crew of six. Others on the dock give offerings
to my new master and join us. We cross the great river.
On that wide flood of peace, I seem to float out of myself
and say farewell to all I am on earth, to all the past
of dead accomplishment, to all that does not matter now.

LXXV.

"We disembark at a mighty city—Waset, called Thebes.
It teems with human dealing, commerce, building, vigorous
at the brink of its legendary time. My master mounts
a donkey wagon waiting for him, not luxurious
but convenient. I walk behind with the other servants.
The sun is at its zenith, and I am but a being
aware of his attention in a time of no shadows.

LXXVI.

"Through the city we walk, the river to the right, no thoughts
intruding, the mind marveling at what the eyes receive.
We move past the great temple to the end of the complex
then turn round to enter it from the south, up the causeway
of Ipetisut, The Most Select of Places. Behold!
There is no other destination. Across the desert,
across the river, across lifetimes, here I am in God.

LXXVII.

"Once in the temple complex, I am taken to a room
where my head and body are shaved, my teeth cleaned, my nails trimmed,
all my skin scrubbed with a pungent solution that leaves me
red and puckered. A cotton garment, simple but refined,
is given me to wear, and a light headdress and cloth band.
Then I am escorted to a grand kitchen where a man
dressed as I am is pointed out to me. I stand and watch.

LXXVIII.

"The man enters bent under all the sacks of raw produce
he can carry, then exits under sacks filled with refuse.
Back and forth he goes, no haste, his movements slow and secure.
Such is my work for six months on, and from it I learn much:
how to move and breathe, how to balance the body's effort,
how to keep the mind clear of useless thoughts, how to sustain
the sacred attention that transforms mere breath into prayer.

LXXIX.

"When my readiness satisfies the Gods, the accident
that brings my elevation is allowed to come to pass.
A bowl of syrup slips from the hands of a man whose feet
slide on the liquid, sending him headlong into a wall,
splitting his skull, leaving him unconscious. Before help comes,
I staunch the wound and restore the rhythm of his breathing.
By then I have the words to say, 'I am a physician.'

LXXX.

"Within days I am transferred to the temple hospital
where I serve out the next thirty months of my indenture.
I come to understand that on the river's western bank
I sold myself, a seven-years servant, to a great man,
the Third Prophet of the temple, third in line to the High Priest.
I see him rarely, his visits quiet and inconspicuous;
his work, they say, secret, crucial to the future of Thebes.

LXXXI.

"My work is satisfying but limited: setting bones,
salving and cauterizing wounds, manipulating spines.
I am not a surgeon, and my knowledge of healing drugs
is small compared to the masters' here; I am treated well,
but it is clear I will not be trained in their solemn arts.
I perform my duties faithfully and accumulate
the vocabulary of my trade. These are happy years.

LXXXII.

"Here I must pause again," said Carroll. "I apologize
for the strange fragmentary nature of the narrative,
but I am giving to you what has been given to me."
"But you have researched this material. You have placed it
in known history, have you not?" Anamusa wondered.
"I have tried," said Carroll, but history is often dim
and sketchy, a context created from a shard of fact."

LXXXIII.

"But you have identified your story's setting as Thebes
in the Second Intermediary," Jules reaffirmed.
"So Egypt is divided, the lower under the rule
of the Hyksos, the 'Asians-in-Egypt' you spoke about."
"Yes," said Carroll. "And thus Thebes is quietly preparing
for its future greatness in the New Kingdom," Jules reasoned aloud.
"So what is the work the Third Prophet does?" questioned Ruby.

LXXXIV.

"I thank you, Jules, for filling in these helpful facts. I see
them just as you've deduced, but for the nature of the work
the Third Prophet does, I hope you will be patient, Ruby."
"If there's promise in the patience, I'll bear it," she replied.
"There's always promise in patience," Mathilde declared sweetly.
"Patience is the state of ruling the passions," she went on.
"With the passions quieted, what emerges is profound."

LXXXV.

"Perhaps," said Marco, "we can rule our own passions and let
the profundity of Carroll's tale emerge. Please go on."
"Thank you," said Carroll. "I hope there's promise in it for you."
He resumed. "One morning I arrive to find my master
waiting for me. From the smell of the astringents, I know
that he has just been bathed and groomed. His garment is spotless,
but his body is in pain, as battered as it is clean.

LXXXVI.

"He tells me he has just returned from a hard journey,
hard because he's unaccustomed to riding and sleeping
on the ground. 'I am not a soldier,' he says with a smile.
He says he's heard I have healing hands, that he needs treatment,
that he hopes I will be gracious and generous to him.
I am stunned at his courtesy, honored by his presence.
A great man seeks simplicity and uses simple words.

LXXXVII.

"His years of training make him a perfect patient. He knows
how to surrender to my hands and release the clenched pain,
how to breathe to meet the changing pressure, how to keep me
well aware of my own effects with subtle sighs and groans.
Even as I realign his body, he teaches me
by his presence to be present. He shows me pressure points
in neck and lower spine which act as valves for heart and mind.

LXXXVIII.

"As he prepares to leave, I hear myself ask the question,
'Where do you go and what do you do to so strain yourself?'
Even as the words emerge, I feel embarrassed by them.
'Excuse me,' I say. 'I am beyond my place. Forgive.'
He gazes at me, his eyes soft, without admonishment.
'We go north on these quests. Say I am a smuggler for God.'
He thanks me, and from that day we are joined in destiny.

LXXXIX.

"At first his visits are sporadic, but as months go by
they grow in frequency and reach a regularity
that gives form and purpose to my presence at the temple.
He is under my hands many times before the courage
comes to ask more about his project. I am astounded
when he openly divulges his daring endeavor:
'We are moving Egypt's sacred keys from Memphis to Thebes.'

XC.

"He continues, revealing a labor that could arise
only in a mind comprehending the deepest secrets
of man's purpose. 'Consolidating, reformulating
the great knowledge will elicit a king strong enough
to drive out the Asians from the north and regenerate
godly ways in Egypt. I go to Cusae to retrieve
what priests in Memphis have hidden in Heliopolis.'

XCI.

"'You must understand, my boy,'—I am shocked to be called such—
'the knowledge cannot be expunged or man himself will die.
It is our job to make a new text, not from new knowledge
nor from our own inspiration, but from what is proven.
We must give it a shape and refinement that ages hence
can use, but the substance will be as it has always been.
The Gods have led you here and connected you to this work.'

XCII.

"I am astonished at his words, humbled into silence.
He leaves, noting his return in six days, offering me
his certainty. 'Your role will be made clear as it is lived.'
Upon his return, my duties are expanded. I keep
his person healthy, his schedule ordered, his rooms tidy.
At every task of his priestly role, I am at his side
ready for what comes, protecting the space, witnessing all.

XCIII.

"The trips to Cusae come to a close. The material
is gathered and complete. The work of composing begins.
In a large room converted to our use are assembled
scribes, scroll making craftsmen, their slaves, students of the priesthood,
guards and woodcarvers—all under my master's direction.
The project goes on for months and months. Nothing is written
that my master does not approve. I observe and obey.

XCIV.

"One evening he holds me at table after dinner.
He speaks to me solemnly, with both love and heaviness.
'You are not of our order; thus an initiation
is not possible, but I want you to learn this Scripture.
Learn it not as spells and orations but as the symbols
of the battle that each instructed man must wage to claim
himself, to know himself, and to be unified with God.'

XCV.

"As much as I have seen, I don't yet understand his words,
but soon he begins to instruct me with the images
the craftsmen have fashioned to illustrate the orations.
At first these pictures seem quaint, but as my grasp of them grows,
I am more impressed by their perfect allegories.
'How do our craftsmen devise these so precisely?' I ask.
'I tell them what to draw,' my master says, 'and thus they learn.'

XCVI.

"I think I see what's happening here. It is like Moses
distilling and bringing forth the ten—the Decalogue—then
instructing the scribes in its meaning," Anamusa said.
"I was thinking of Bernard and the cathedral builders—
one great Heaven-guided mind preserving and instructing."
"Take care, Mathilde." Marco smiled gently to admonish
his wife. "We're sliding into an imagined history."

XCVII.

"O, you are right, my dear," sighed Mathilde. "How embarrassing
to be lured away by one of Carroll's Egyptian spells."
"Actually the spells keep one from being lured away."
'Thank you Jules," said Carroll politely. "Now I am concerned.
The premise of this story is so dubious and faint,
it tempts us to imagination. Perhaps I should close."
"What doesn't tempt us to imagination?" Ruby asked.

XCVIII.

"What do you mean, Ruby?" wondered Anamusa mildly.
"If Carroll abandons his story, something else will sing
the Siren song," Ruby answered. 'As I'm coming to see,
our minds if not restrained will always lapse to wandering."
"You are right," said Marco. "We are the danger, not the tale."
"There's your verdict, Carroll," Jules chuckled. "Please do continue.
We understand you make no claims for your fanciful plot."

XCIX.

"Thank you," Carroll said. "Allow me a minute to anchor
my mind to task. The years do not make this telling less strange."
With that he fixed his gaze, and breathing rhythmically resumed.
"I learn the internal human scale of the great cosmos
to which the spells refer. Heaven is a state as is hell,
and all the Gods and monsters, images of animals,
are but the world within craving order under the sun."

C.

"The work is always the same: Divine Presence, the High God,
most often in the symbol of a sacred conception,
quickens in a pure heart the longing for liberation.
From this miraculous union, the Steward son is born,
destined to die in the selfless suffering of return.
All the symbols and spells enact this drama of return.
To Presence, to Conscious Godhead, the story is return.

CI.

"I am my master's helper in all his public duties.
Though I cannot be initiated, I learn the rites
by heart and come to know their inner meaning. As time moves,
I find my life turning inside out; ritual events
become reminders to cultivate consciousness within
and groom silent presence. Great contentment overtakes me
as the purpose of my life—of all life—secures itself.

CII.

"As I learn this new way of life, my master educates
the priests in the prayers he has collected and in their use.
Over time, the new canon—though not really new at all—
penetrates the ceremonies and becomes the custom.
There is resistance from older members of the order,
both priests and prosperous men, for whom the old fragment spells
and the order's high status are too comforting to lose.

CIII.

"Then they lose all in protecting nothing," says my master.
"The new knowledge does not violate but completes the old."
Respected men, even priests, depart—where is there to go?—
and slowly the order is purified of their tired hearts
which can go no further in this life. It is hard, piercing
to watch favored men forsake their gift. May Heaven's mercy
find them down the spiral of time. The story is return.

CIV.

"Once, following a rite for the Opening of the Mouth,
I asked my master about the meaning of this ritual.
'I have shown you the pressure point in the back of the neck.
That point opens the throat—an aspect of the narrow gate—
allowing the fine fire waiting in the kindled heart to rise
to the eye and the crown. In mind activity, the tongue
sticks against the roof of the mouth, blocking the fire's ascent."

CV.

"'This I know,' I told him, 'but the dead man and his children
for whom you performed today know nothing of this teaching.'
'For them, it is religion, a great structure of belief
that gives meaning to the world. It is what most men require.'
'And we let them trust in a lie?' I ask, my heart sinking.
'Religion hides then dramatizes the truth in story.
It is not a lie but a level of understanding.'

CVI.

"He goes on, 'And from religion comes civilization,
and the raw earth is made a garden for the growth of souls.'
'But who determines which ones are entrusted with the truth?'
At this he points his finger skyward. 'That day in the market
when I met you, reflected light from a perfume bottle
formed a circle in the center of your brow, a clear sign
for me to teach you, a lone, lost foreigner. I obey.'

CVII.

"He would say no more, and in truth there is no more to say.
Under his clear guidance, the new version of orations
and utterances infiltrate the ancient practices,
first carved on wooden coffins then refined to scribal scrolls.
I learn the sacred numbers and, though awkwardly at first,
employ them in my private meditation. The trickle
of presence climbing to my higher parts steadily grows.

CVIII.

"As does Thebes, though imperceptibly at first. Holding fast
her independence, she profits, however loyalties
north and south shift and realign. By the end
of my indenture, she is thriving. Her alliances
come on terms more and more favorable, her trade expands,
and with both come money for arms. Growing to abundance,
the flow of tribute gold surpasses that from her own mines.

CIX.

"A month from the end of my contracted service, I ask
my master if I may renew. He looks at me kindly
and puts his hands on my shoulders. 'No renewal, my boy.
If you stay in Thebes to do your practice, I can arrange
a marriage with an honorable girl. That is the last thing
I can offer you. You have enough from my instruction
if it is your fate to keep your heart afire unto death.'

CX.

"To take a woman again, to be but a householder—
for days I am shocked and desolate at the idea.
I want to stay at my master's side, even if he speaks
not another word for my instruction. Slowly my will
to do my own work, to spur the growth of my own soul,
finds itself, and the temple girl my master finds for me
is pleased at the prospect and promises obedience.

CXI.

"On my thirty-seventh birthday, I am married once more.
We are moved to a small house in a military camp
a few miles down river from Thebes. I am a physician
to the soldiers—setting bones, salving wounds, realigning
the spines of rough officers who must be taught to receive
healing treatment. In the job I am content, but my heart
is full of longing for the presence of my master's eye.

CXII.

"One day I'm called to the edge of the fortification
where a tunnel has collapsed into a hidden cavern.
A soldier, his head hit by falling rock, lies unconscious
at the brink of a great dark descent no one's torch can find
the bottom of. Into the tunnel, through its serpentine path
I go, till the light of the sky is but a memory.
There he is, stretched out. By his breath I know he's all but dead.

CXIII.

"And there I am looking at myself looking at the corpse.
I'm kneeling over, suspended between a distant light
I can return to and an endless darkness. The captain
stands over us. 'You must know what to do,' he firmly says,
and his words echo once, twice, three times down the dark belly
of the cavern. I examine the man. His back is whole,
nothing broken in his middle. We carry him back up.

CXIV.

"I know as I am living this it is a sign from God.
I am alert and full of consciousness as we ascend
into the light and lay the man down gently on the ground.
I apply a rhythmic pressure to his chest to deepen
his breathing, and in a few moments he begins to cough.
In an hour, he knows himself again, though in throbbing pain,
and I—I know what I must do with the rest of my life.

CXV.

"Not long thereafter, my wife tells me she has conceived.
A part of me is glad, even as another part longs
to be in the Temple and another part to move on.
A thing of parts held together by will, my earthly work
faithfully done—beneath this level I must never fall.
But at my best, the fuel having risen to my eye,
I am no part of earth, but silent presence looking on.

CXVI.

"I work a year of days, see a strong son born, listen less
and less to the urgent lies of my lower nature.
My heart grows pure, its lifting unrestrained and past desire.
The army grows, the numbers recommended to my art
increase, mostly those of rank seeking relief from worries
they have brought on themselves feeding self-importance. They
grip the air as if their spears were ever in their hands.

CXVII.

"One day a general under my hands begins to talk,
telling me of deep disruption in the temple order—
the First Prophet suddenly dead, the Second now dismissed
for sedition, my master first in line to be High Priest.
Now I know I will not see him again, his life taken
by his fated task, his days absorbed in ceremony.
I remind the general to be still if he would heal.

CXVIII.

"My wife is taken up in motherhood. She has a role,
an endeavor of meaning, a center of gravity.
The boy is mine and not mine. He bears me a resemblance
in the shoulders and the skull, but his muscles are more dense,
like my father's, and he strains to pull himself up to walk.
Our acquaintances, mostly soldiers, love his fierce spirit.
It takes no special vision to see he'll be a soldier.

CIX.

At this point Carroll set his feet and slowly stood and stretched.
"But one episode remains," he said, "and it's better told
if I gather myself a bit." By then the momentum
of his tale had captured all of us, and we were eager
to continue, but his pause gave us opportunity
to recollect ourselves, to relax our bated breathing
and to make ready to receive what we could not predict.

CXX.

Around us, the airport and Philadelphia itself
had returned to full activity, and in the ancient
configuration of our unity, we were a crystal
of light—tiny, to be sure, but unbreakable—afloat
on a swirling ocean of noisy human business.
We had only to meet each other's eyes to feel the joy
of what we had made of our stranded hours, so soon to end.

CXXI.

"Let us return and finish well," Carroll said with welcome;
then he drew a deep breath, released it and resumed his tale.
"Shortly after my son's fifth birthday, I begin to note
persistent piercing pain deep in the left side of my throat,
not an inflammation, but more the sharp twinge of something
impinging on a nerve. Despite my knowledge of muscle
and sinew, it is beyond my skill to ease the stinging.

CXXII.

"Normally I never trade on my acquaintanceships,
but in this case fearing something dire, I go upriver
to the great complex and seek a private consultation
with the temple's head physician, whose mastery I trust.
He agrees to see me, and in his teaching theatre
examines me. 'It is as you thought, a mass on a nerve,
a fast growing tumor.' His gaze is soft, his voice soothing.

CXXIII.

"He continues, 'I can excise it before it limits
your shoulder and your hand and disables you from your work,
but within a year it will grow back and spread as it grows.
It is fatal. You will weaken and waste and then succumb.
I am sorry my friend, but the truth is best, even now.'
I receive this news without surprise, but then a great shock:
I turn and there, silent in the doorway, is my master.

CXXIV.

"'I was told you were here. Heaven has reunited us
at a most auspicious moment,' he says without pity.
'It will require all your skill and learning, all I've taught you,
to exploit your dying for an eternal victory.
'I do not fear it,' I tell him as we move to embrace.
'I am blessed with time to work, time to master readiness.'
'Indeed a blessing,' he agrees. 'You have Heaven's favor.'

CXXV.

"So there I stand between two masters, one of the body,
the other of the soul and space and time, both promising
to help me mount the final stairs to a meaningful death.
I am told to return in a week for the surgery,
assured that the inhalants will reduce the pain. Borne up
in this triad of truth, uniquely present, is a taste
of deathless being, certain and prophetic. I depart.

CXXVI.

"The surgery succeeds in buying time, perhaps a year
of nearly normal function. My wife and son sense something
is different, limited now, but the change is subtle
and easily buffered in the daily round of habit.
I practice prayers relentlessly, ascending and diving
deep into the unknown, residing there. Why could I not live
this way before? We need the circling predatory moon.

CXXVII.

"I become a comfort to my patients, consolation
for their hearts. They come with broken bones, muscle masses warped
and inflamed, spines misaligned, but they leave deeply healed, new.
To men whose work forbids surrender, I give permission
to surrender, if only for an hour; my hands have not
their former strength, but my eyes—open, soft, deep and limpid—
dissolve all human care with their assuring radiance.

CXXVIII.

"I visit the physician twice in the year given me
by his skill. My master attends both appointments. No words
are needed. We share the same understanding and resolve.
By the end of that year, my body is diminishing,
beginning to waste: first the massy muscles of the legs
and buttocks, then the arms and shoulders; last and grudgingly
goes the visceral flesh, the vital surpluses vanishing.

CXXIX.

"When I tell my wife, she is not surprised; she is not blind
to life before her, but she asks why I so long withheld
the truth. Her questions pain me, but I dare not dwell on it.
Soon the boy will be in school. Already the favorite
of the soldiers, he will help his mother, look after her,
learning manhood by mimicking it. My place will be filled
by his pretense or the welcome of another husband.

CXXX.

"The final phase begins. My shrunken arms forfeit their strength.
I cannot stand more than an hour. I must resign my job.
It is the worst of a merciless midsummer. The sun
commands the cowering world; its unbuffered radiance
unbearable. Requiring water and shade, life retracts.
My stools show blood, more and more copious its fatal flow.
I do not know the hour, but the day arrives most clearly.

CXXXI.

"At my behest, my son runs to have the captain send us
a man with a cart. Ibhan arrives at my door barely
an hour later with his broad familiar smile, ignorant
of his errand. I cannot lift my son to embrace him,
so he mounts a chair to receive his father's forehead kiss.
My comprehending wife restrains herself from all display
of passion. I can see she has surrendered all to God.

CXXXII.

"It is still early morning when we depart. The sun climbs
aggressively to its throne. I ask Ibhan to take me
to the river and give him money to hire a ferry.
The cool breeze from the river, its clean uplifting fragrance,
welcomes us. Ibhan helps me from the cart and goes to find
a boat. He returns with a grizzled ferryman, toothless
and leathery, a man who does not see beyond his job.

CXXXIII.

"I give Ibhan his instructions and he becomes alarmed.
I tell him I will cross alone, that he's to wait two hours
before following. From a landmark he knows well, an hour
of walking west will find me. I hand him a sealed package
containing a folded shroud. He will deduce what to do.
'But you are too weak to go alone,' he protests. I smile.
'I am never alone. I am instructed in each step.'

CXXXIV.

"I leave him, puzzled but calmed, and follow the ferryman.
The crossing is smooth, the white light on the water dazzling.
On the other shore, I discard my things, even my staff,
and getting my bearings, begin to walk west. There is pain,
but it is not mine; there is shortness of breath and weakness
in stride, but the body obeys. It must be exhausted,
taken beyond all strength to resist, all will of its own.

CXXXV.

"When there's no more need to walk, I turn to the perfect East.
Above is the sun, so definite, and so pervasive
in radiance. To my right is the huge temple complex,
far away but dominant, casting long morning shadows
from the other shore. I disrobe and find the position
that completes the triad by which instructed men return.
Both focused and distinct, I die looking into the sun."

CXXXVI.

With these words, Carroll ended his tale. He looked up and moved
his eyes around our order, pausing lightly on each one of us.
His face lifted and brightened, his back stretched, and both his arms
extended out then up above his head. A smile appeared
on his lips. "I am finished," he said in rising radiance.
It was late morning, nearing noon, and as the great bustle
around us re-entered our ears, we savored completion.

CXXXVII.

"What a marvelous story, Carroll," Anamusa chimed.
"Very intriguing," Jules added, "but have you verified
that this Egyptian character is somehow you, Carroll?"
"I don't know how I would do that, Jules," Carroll responded.
"What I know is that I possess this record of a life,
and I have offered it to you as it emerged to me.
It concludes our game well, I think. I make no other claim."

CXXXVIII.

"And if our game is well concluded, what now?" Ruby asked.
"We are ready to fly," said Marco. "With six fine stories
we have shouldered aside whatever could keep us earthbound."
"Our bodies are quiet," Anamusa said. "A long night
of congenial work has exhausted our restlessness.
And our minds are clean; that is, whatever new thoughts sprout there
are observable. We sit at home, looking out, composed."

CXXXIX.

We all sat silent demanding nothing of the moment
but our attention to it. The great interior space
of the terminal was filled with the morning light flooding
in from the windows, and the teeming movement of the crowd
around us, its burgeoning activity and brute noise,
made of our kind configuration an island of peace,
as we'd made of ourselves, each and all, a sanctuary.

CXL.

After some time, Anamusa posed a question, "A thought
keeps returning, demanding explanation, so I ask:
how did we forsake the device of framing the stories?"
We all looked at each other, as if a single mind
preparing a reasoned response. Jules was the first to speak.
"Remember, Ana, that I told my tale in character,
abandoning the point of view that could construct a frame."

CXLI.

"You asked this question once before, did you not?" asked Ruby.
"I did," said Ana, "but we never quite came to an answer."
"I think we are the answer," said Carroll. In unison,
three or four crisp voices wondered aloud, "What do you mean?"
"To be fair," said Carroll, "Some of the stories did have frames."
"And some did not," said Ana quickly. Carroll continued,
Exactly. So the whole was both in and out of the frame."

CXLII.

"Are you playing on our dear Walt Whitman?" Ana queried.
"I don't understand," said Ruby. Ana said, "Did he not
call himself 'both in and out of the game?' I thought Carroll
was joking on a passage that certainly describes us."
"I am not so clever," said Carroll, "but thank you for the thought.
Actually, I was referring to the convention
in School art of objects extending past a framing line."

CXLIII.

"Like Gabriel's horn in the great Persian miniature,
or Christ's foot in the Ravenna mosaic?" Ana asked.
"Precisely," answered Carroll. "It was a code suggesting
that the character was out of time, free of the limit."
"Just as our efforts take us out of time," agreed Marco.
"Ah, how wonderful!" gleamed Mathilde. "I believe," said Carroll,
"that we've now come full circle, the end to the beginning."

CXLIV.

"Please explain," said Ruby. "Do remember," Carroll went on
"that many hours ago, it was earnest conversation
about being out of time that spurred us to the fine game
we've just completed." "I had forgotten," Jules admitted.
"I remember only because I was the one doing
most of the talking," Carroll laughed. "I was just stitching thoughts
and look what the Gods had us weave to wear for a garment."

CXLV.

"A garment of virtue!" Mathilde exclaimed. "Through our efforts
over the last few hours, we have cleaned and clothed our stewards."
"And kept alive a colony of presence," added Jules.
"We have been returning home the whole time," Carroll affirmed.
"So the frame of time could not hold us," said Anamusa.
"Now I understand and see the hand of Heaven writing.
"The work informs our thoughts," said Marco. "We're ready to fly."

CXLVI.

"It's hard to keep pace with these epiphanies," said Ruby.
She turned her eyes to me as if in appeal, then she smiled.
"Hoisted from the frame they speak of into the now," she said.
"We have a lot of catching up to do, don't we, William?"
"We do, " I answered. "We're being taken by a whirlwind
and asked to have patience. The present is our only choice.
Instruction from the Gods leaves no room for anything else."

CXLVII.

At that moment came the shock of hearing my name announced
with directions to report to the passenger check in.
"Ah, our departure has begun, William," Carroll noted,
"and you are the first. So it is true, the last shall be first."
I stood, and their faces, upturned in unity and love,
offered me a wordless benevolence. My heart opened,
and filling with their overbrimming love, I nearly swooned.

CXLVIII.

"I'll be back in just a minute," I managed to utter
and went to the desk. I was told there was one seat open
on Flight 604, leaving from Gate 18, six gates on.
"You need to hurry," said the attendant, a young lady
whose nametag read 'Maria'. "They're holding the plane for you."
"And what of my friends? I asked. She assured me, "They'll be called
one by one. Everyone gets in the air and home today."

CXLIX.

I turned ready to rush back to them only to find them
clustered behind me, waiting, their six faces radiant.
"Let us walk you to the gate, my boy," said Anamusa.
She led the way. I walked behind with Ruby to my right.
Behind us walked the other four; as a pyramid we moved
in procession up the hall, unified in breath and step.
As we arrived at the sixth gate, they blessed my departure.

CL.

To each I gave a kiss, and an embrace and a moment
in each other's eye. I was aware of warm tears spilling
gently down, and in my heart mixed gratitude and longing.
To the very edge I went then turned and found their faces,
holding doubled attention, sending me aloft with love.
Over the threshold through the tunnel onto the plane I went,
and taking my right place, rose silently into the sky.

William's Envoi: *Four In-Flight Meditations*

I.

I am aloft above thirty thousand feet, soaring home.
How easy it is, even here looking out this window,
to lapse from presence into the shallow meanderings,
the meaningless motions of thought. Man prefers the darkness
of individual mind, his own mocking universe,
to the true light of God, so bright as to annihilate
all peeping vanities, all petty claims, all names, all words.

I give thanks for the instruction I've received, the secret
which is no secret: that in presence we return to God,
and know God, and become part of God. Thus the great teaching!
So simple is the truth, right here before us, a marvel
that we must be taught it. And the next second we lose it
to the coils of the tempting mind. One must give one's whole life
to the practice of the present, to return and return.

There is nothing finer on earth, no greater victory
than the congregation of instructed men, joined in love,
partners in remembering, making beauty, knowing God.
In their garden are the fruits to refresh fading mankind;
at the corners of their city are the fountains
from which flow the sacred waters of regeneration.
I am returning there, flying home in mindful silence.

II.

Who are the Gods but former men like us now transcended,
their astral selves made sufficient for independent life
in the dimension of eternity? Who are the Gods
but those who practiced the miraculous alchemy?
The labor of remembering oneself in the present,
the transformation of suffering by accepting it,
such is the earthly life of a man becoming a God.

Who are the Gods but those who have borne civilization
on their shoulders? In the cloister or in the capital,
in the artist's studio or in the poet's old chair,
chosen by the older Gods, overwatched and directed,
the new Gods fashion themselves for eternity and leave
us the fruits of their influence. The universe runs down,
but the cord of conscious work ascends to the Absolute.

The effort to be present is the only real praying.
Only in the present are Gods accessible to men,
and without their help there is no continuing; we move
with brute muscles in the blind steps of instinct to our graves
unless the Gods place us in the line of their instruction,
and we give up everything else to stay there. Returning
and returning through life and lives, we become eternal.

III.

A poem must be made of this, a poem Heaven owns.
There's no great epic here, no mythic fight or cosmic sweep,
no founding of a race, no grand heroic destiny—
just friends telling tales of such things, brief excerpts of glory
and present will bound in a loving configuration.
But all the tellers are instructed men, feeling the breath
of higher being in their tales, in their unchosen words.

A poem must be made of this, but am I up to it?
Whose help can I invoke? What transcended man will guide me,
prompt the plan and hold me to the chair when I would leave it
for some manufactured duty or mindless amusement?
If there's a better venture for my time, an idea
more worthy, I cannot devise it, but aspiration
without higher help soon breathes shallow and forgets itself.

I would honor our Teacher and my friends, and say nothing
ignoble or untrue, and in that I need not but tell
what happened: our little gathering was a testament
to our Teacher's conscious love and thus attracted Heaven.
Can I trust that attention — mine and Heaven's — to remain
and carry an obscure task of measured inspirations
through to its luminous completion? A poem must be made.

IV.

I am humbled by how often I must be reminded
to return, to regrip the present. Holding the present
is of all things in life the most important, but it slips
from my hand like water, like air does mindfulness disperse.
To abandon the body bag of false identity,
to become the present, is the aim of life, but what hope
of that do I have if I cannot remember to be?

Thus the work of friendship, and the aim of all sacred texts,
and the form of Heaven's love—to remind us, to bring us
home from the mind's indulgent wanderings and help us stand
above the mortal flow of change, the temptation of time.
I must be brought back a dozen dozen times a day,
a hundred angel lifts my fragile soul requires to stay
above the flood. When will my steps be steadfast and not sink?

Our descent has just been announced. I refasten my belt
and prepare for earth's pressure and jolt. The flight is spent,
the weight returning; already I feel the human clench.
I am young in this work, a child in the Way of the Child,
yet childish distress, however valid, is but distraction.
The sea of confusion will swirl on without my dark thoughts
pulling me in; the clamor of men does not need my cries.

Divine Presence is always here, patient, accessible
to will through the laws in which Heaven has instructed men.
Surrender to presence, submit and be, silently, be.